Resource Book
Purification and Enlightenment
Year A,B,C

Foundations in Faith

Bob Duggan • Carol Gura

Rita Ferrone • Gael Gensler

Steve Lanza • Donna Steffen

Maureen A. Kelly

RESOURCES FOR CHRISTIAN LIVING™

Allen, Texas

President
Kim Duty

Publisher
Maryann Nead

Authors
Bob Duggan • Carol Gura
Rita Ferrone • Gael Gensler
Steve Lanza • Donna Steffen

Product Manager
Maureen A. Kelly

Editorial Director
Ed DeStefano

Editors
Linda Hartley, Patricia Classick

Book Design
Pat Bracken

Senior Production Editor
Laura Fremder

Cover Design
Karen McDonald

Nihil Obstat
Rev. Msgr. Glenn D. Gardner, J.C.D.
Censor Librorum

Imprimatur
Most Rev. Charles V. Grahmann
Bishop of Dallas

December 30, 1997

The Nihil Obstat and Imprimatur are official declarations that the material reviewed is free of doctrinal or moral error. No implication is contained therein that those granting the Nihil Obstat and Imprimatur agree with the contents, opinions, or statements expressed.

Send all inquiries to:
RCL • Resources for Christian Living
200 Bethany Drive
Allen, Texas 75002-3804

Toll free   800-822-6701
Fax   800-688-8356

Printed in the United States of America

12709   ISBN 0-7829-0763-6

1 2 3 4 5   02 01 00 99 98

Contents

Introduction

One of the great fallacies of our Western, technological mind-set is the idea that time is a quantity like any other, able to be measured with precision, the mere marking of sequential units. In this view, all time is the same, and designated units of time are best distinguished quantitatively (more or less, longer or shorter), not qualitatively. Our biblical and liturgical tradition knows better, however, that the true human measure of time distinguishes time more by quality than quantity. "A thousand years in your eyes are merely a yesterday," the psalmist proclaims (Psalm 90:4, NAB); and, in the rhythms of the liturgical cycle, we believe that past and future meet in a timeless "now" whenever the mysteries of salvation are made present in the Church's worship.

Sacred time, as an experience of the eternal "now," grants access to the divinity, and from that encounter one always emerges transformed. The early Christians, like their Jewish ancestors, carved out special feasts and seasons during which they commemorated—and rendered present—the saving power of God that they had experienced throughout the ages. Observing Sunday as the "Lord's Day," on which they gathered for a meal in memory of the dying and rising of Jesus, was the earliest Christian attempt to claim as sacred a segment of time which the rest of the world viewed like any other: just another workday in the Roman Empire. Commitment to share in that sacred time of eucharistic gathering—even at the risk of one's life—soon came to be recognized as the key to Christian identity. Regular participation clearly resulted in the transformation of those who gathered.

In the decision of the bishops at the Second Vatican Council to restore the ancient catechumenate with its special times and seasons, we have witnessed that this impulse to carve out time as sacred and transformative continues to flourish twenty centuries after the first Christians gathered in secret for their weekly Eucharist. In the *Rite of Christian Initiation of Adults,* (RCIA), the Church has identified one particular stage of the catechumenal process as "a time for spiritual recollection in preparation for the celebration of the paschal mystery" (RCIA, 138). The Rite calls this time the Period of Purification and Enlightenment, and directs that it generally coincide with the liturgical season traditionally known as Lent. This manual hopes to give parish catechumenal teams a feel for the nature of this period and to offer resources that will help them make their community's experience of purification and enlightenment deeply transformative, not only for the catechumens and candidates but for all in the community.

Part one of this manual, consisting of three chapters, gives an overview of the Period of Purification and Enlightenment, describes the journey of the elect and the candidates through this period, and offers concrete suggestions for ways that the parish community can become thoroughly involved in the baptismal focus of this season. Part two consists of resources for the catechist and team pertaining to three types of events: weekly gatherings, preparation sessions for the Scrutinies and Penitential Rite, and retreats. Finally, there is an appendix which includes handouts that are correlated with the various sessions and events described and may be duplicated for participants.

The weekly gatherings for which Scripture background and session plans are provided take the place of the catechetical sessions that were used in the catechumenate period. The Scripture background begins with exegetical material, goes on to identify and describe key images in the readings, and concludes with a brief summary statement on the message of that day's Word, leading into the session that follows. In keeping with the character of this period as a time of retreat and spiritual recollection rather than a time of catechetical instruction, the sessions are called "Initial Reflection" (for the half-hour time period immediately following the dismissal from the liturgy) and "Extended Reflection" (for the longer period spent either on Sunday or on another day of the week). Scripture background and "Initial Reflection" sessions for Holy Thursday and Good Friday are also included.

Whenever there are elect preparing for baptism, the three Scrutinies are celebrated and the readings for Year A are used on the Third, Fourth, and Fifth Sunday of Lent. The session plans reflect this usage, and the experience of the elect in the Scrutinies is stressed in the sessions for these Sundays of Year A. Sessions for Years B and C are provided for those occasions when a parish has only baptized candidates preparing for Confirmation and Eucharist. In such a case, the Scrutinies would not be celebrated; therefore, the readings would be taken from whatever year of the lectionary cycle the Church is currently celebrating: A, B, or C.

On the Second Sunday of Lent, when the Penitential Rite for the baptized candidates is usually celebrated in the dioceses of the United States, the session plans for Years A, B, and C all include reference to this rite. If a parish has *only* elect and no candidates, or if you are in an episcopal conference outside of the United States which does not include this Penitential Rite for candidates as one of its options, the exercises relating to this rite should be omitted by the one leading the session.

There are options offered for each Scrutiny and Penitential Rite preparation session. Any of them may be used. Members of the parish may participate in these sessions, as well as the elect and candidates with their godparents and sponsors, or be done simply in the group of those preparing for the Easter sacraments. Scrutiny and Penitential Rite preparation involving the whole parish is highly recommended. Such preparation sessions may be scheduled once or several times in preparation for each of these events. Likewise, the retreat resources are flexible and arranged for maximum adaptability to individual needs and circumstances. Day-long and weekend retreat plans are offered; and for those parishes which have greater time limitations, individual parts of the retreats described may be used for an evening or half-day retreat.

In short, an abundance of materials have been offered to help you and others in your parish to experience this time in all its fullness. Having "set out with us on the road that leads to the glory of Easter" (RCIA, 136A), may the elect and all who walk with them truly experience the Lenten season as sacred time.

PART ONE

Chapter 1

Understanding the Period of Purification and Enlightenment

*I*n order to appreciate the nature of the Period of Purification and Enlightenment called for by the *Rite of Christian Initiation of Adults,* one must have some knowledge of the origins and history of Lent.

Origins and History of Lent

The earliest rhythm of gathering by the first generation of Christians was weekly, their celebration of the Lord's Supper on the day of his Resurrection. Quite soon, however, they began to observe an annual commemoration of his dying and rising in conjunction with the Jewish Passover. Practices differed from place to place, and centuries passed before there was substantial agreement on the most appropriate calendar to follow in observing the *Pascha Domini* (the Lord's passover from death to life); eventually, what we now follow as the way to fix the date of Easter came to be accepted and observed throughout the Christian world. In preparation for that annual feast day, a vigil that involved fasting was observed, but it was not at that time connected to the practice of Christian initiation. (In those earliest times, initiation of new members happened throughout the year.)

It was in the third and especially the fourth and fifth centuries that the Church developed a much more elaborate structure to its liturgical cycle. This was also the period of time during which the rites used to initiate new members underwent a dramatic development. The Edict of Constantine in A.D. 313, which gave public legitimacy to the Christian religion, soon meant that the liturgy was celebrated on a grander and more elaborate scale. This was also the era of massive conversions, which meant that there was need for pastoral structures to form the new converts in the Christian faith. The convergence of all of these factors produced the ancient catechumenate, spread out over a long process of formation, whose distinct stages were marked by rituals that defined the steps of the conversion journey.

The development of what we have come to know as the liturgical year, with its special seasons of Advent, Christmas, Lent, and Easter, also occurred during this time. This is significant because the annual celebration of Easter was eventually chosen as the privileged time for celebrating the final rites of initiation. What had initially been a modest fast for a one-day celebration of the *Pascha Domini* evolved into a longer period—eventually forty days—of preparation for those chosen to be initiated at Easter. Thus, Lent, as it came to be known, was one of the key pastoral structures of the catechumenate aimed at helping the elect make their final preparations for the sacraments of initiation. The character of the time was primarily that of a prebaptismal retreat rather than a time of penance for sins, and the fast prior to celebrating the *Pascha Domini* remained limited to just a day or two leading up to the nighttime vigil of the Resurrection.

Customs varied throughout the regions where Christianity flourished, and in general there was a rich development of rituals that marked and filled this time as a "sacred" season. Something resembling our contemporary Rite of Election marked the beginning of this more intense time of prayer and instruction. Exorcistic rituals, forerunners of our contemporary Scrutinies, were commonly practiced. Expressive rites with catechetical intent—the presentations of the Creed and the Our Father—were developed to accompany the special instructions that the bishop was giving to the elect on a regular basis during this time. The focus of all of this ritual and catechetical activity was the catechumens, and throughout the forty days of Lent the entire Church was involved in supporting, praying for, and walking with the men and women who were preparing to be born again in Christ during the night vigil that lasted until dawn on Easter Sunday morning. For many of the faithful, Easter was the anniversary of their own baptism, and so it was natural that they should use that same time as a period of preparation to renew their commitment to Jesus as the Christ. Thus, the whole Church experienced the baptismal character of Lent and marked the time with rituals and instructions that focused on the meaning of Christian initiation.

Within a few centuries, the Christian faith had spread throughout the Roman Empire. As a result, adult initiation was virtually replaced by infant baptism. Because of the high infant mortality rate and the Church's wide acceptance of Augustine's teaching on original sin, infants came to be baptized soon after birth rather than at Easter. This left Lent, the premier season for baptismal preparation, without a ritual or catechetical focus. Not coincidentally, the decline of adult baptism had been paralleled by the rise of public penance. Quite naturally, the vacuum left by the disappearance of catechumens was filled by the public penitents, and the focus of Lent shifted from initiation to penance. Then, within a few centuries, public penance practiced by a relatively few had in turn been replaced by a more widespread private penance, such as we know today in confession. At that point, the rigors of penitential discipline which had been practiced by the public penitents were replaced by a more modest season of forty days' penance recommended for every Christian. Prayer, fasting, and almsgiving possessed excellent credentials as the classic way of penance (see Matthew, chapter 6), and so these became the ritualized ways of doing penance and the focal point of the Lenten season for the next thousand years.

The Reform of the Second Vatican Council

When one thinks of how deeply ingrained in Christian consciousness the penitential focus of Lent had become over the span of an entire millennium, the momentous nature of the shift mandated at the Second Vatican Council is put into perspective. In the *Constitution on the Sacred Liturgy* (CSL), the bishops of the Council took two decisive actions. First, they ordered the restoration of the ancient catechumenate that had lain dormant for nearly fifteen hundred years (CSL, 64). Second, in their reformation of the liturgical cycle, they directed that greater prominence be given to "the baptismal features which are proper to the Lenten liturgy" (CSL, 109).

The restoration of the catechumenate period was effected after a period of several years' experimentation with the promulgation in 1972 of the *Rite of Christian Initiation of Adults*. That Roman document not only carved out the "sacred time" (i.e., the periods of inquiry, catechumenate, purification and enlightenment, and mystagogia) in which inquirers would become believers but also provided the rituals that would mark and effect their transformation as their conversion experiences unfolded in the midst of the community.

The second step which the bishops at the Council took to change our understanding of the nature of the "sacred time" of Lent as a period of purification and enlightenment was to mandate a reform of the liturgical cycle. That reform was embodied in the publication in 1969 of the *Roman Calendar,* the *Lectionary for Mass,* and the *Sacramentary.* These documents contain a clear shift in their understanding of the nature of the Lenten season. The "General Norms for the Liturgical Year and the Calendar" note that the season of Lent "disposes both catechumens and the faithful to celebrate the paschal mystery: catechumens, through the several stages of Christian initiation; the faithful, through reminders of their own baptism" (27).

The shift reflected in these texts is profound. The task of refocusing a thousand years of Christian consciousness is daunting. Yet, in little more than a single generation, the Church

5th Century and following
◆ Rise of the Order of Penitents:
  • Eventual disappearance of the Order of Catechumens
  • Sackcloth and ashes, prayer and fasting, associated with public penance

7th to 9th Centuries up to the Second Vatican Council
◆ Forty days of Lent becomes a time of penance for the whole Church:
  • Public penance replaced by private penance (confession)
  • Prayer, fasting and almsgiving recommended for all
  • Distinctive fast before the Vigil is lost.
◆ Complete loss of the initiatory character of the forty days
◆ Disappearance of the Order of Penitents

Vatican II to the present
◆ Period of Purification and Enlightenment established as a final preparation for baptism and initiatory rites included in Lent (Election, Scrutinies, Presentations)
◆ Initiatory character of Lent is restored for the whole Church.
◆ Emphasis on the two-day fast prior to the Vigil is restored
◆ Sacraments of Initiation are restored to the Vigil

has already witnessed an amazing transformation. The living presence of catechumens in the midst of parish communities, the power of the rituals which trace their growing discipleship, and the excitement of sponsors and catechists who are called to minister to the conversion experience of others and who find themselves called to deeper faith, have all conspired to produce a rate and depth of change that would have been unthinkable a mere thirty years ago. Lent is steadily recapturing its baptismal focus in the minds and hearts and in the lived experience of Catholics around the world. As the *Rite of Christian Initiation of Adults* is implemented more fully and more faithfully in parish after parish and diocese after diocese, the fondest hopes of the bishops at the Second Vatican Council are steadily being realized. We turn now to a closer look at the Rite to understand better its vision of the Period of Purification and Enlightenment.

The Vision of the Rite

The best place to go for an understanding of what the Period of Purification and Enlightenment is all about is the *Rite of Christian Initiation of Adults* itself. In the prayers and rituals prescribed for this period, and especially in the introductory notes—both to those rituals and to the period as a whole—the full vision of the period is articulated. It is also important to remember the larger context of the entire catechumenal journey, of which the Period of Purification and Enlightenment is but a part. The catechumen or candidate has by this time been involved in the process for many months or even years, and a positive discernment has been made as to his or her readiness for full initiation. This means that what began as an "initial conversion" (RCIA, 6) has now matured to the point of the individual being judged ready to assume fully the burdens of discipleship. All that remains is to undergo the prebaptismal retreat of forty days, together with the rituals that are at its heart.

There is a certain nuance here that is important not to miss. In the Rite of Election, we celebrate God's choice of the elect as well as the elect's acceptance of God's call. The Church affirms the mature conversion that has brought the catechumen to this point. But, at the same time, participation in this period is seen as a necessary step in order that the developing conversion experience might be brought to full maturity. Something decisive is meant to happen in the course of this retreat time, something without which one's conversion would not be complete. That is the point of the Rite's insistence, for example, on the importance of participating in all of the Scrutinies. The Scrutinies are so central to the full conversion of the elect that the Rite requires specific permission from the local ordinary "to dispense, on the basis of some serious obstacle, one scrutiny or extraordinary circumstances, even from two" (RCIA, 34.3). These are the subtle cues by which the Rite indicates that this period of time is meant

---

Purification and Enlightenment in the Vision of the Rite

◆ A decisive time of final preparation and spiritual transformation
◆ Importance of ritual experience (Election, Scrutinies, Presentations)
◆ Involvement of the entire community in the preparation for, or renewal of, Baptism
◆ Focus on purification, balanced by emphasis on enlightenment

to be a decisive, transforming part of the entire catechumenal journey. The challenge to a parish community, of course, is to implement the vision of the Rite in its fullness so that the Period of Purification and Enlightenment will make an indelible impression on the elect.

As subsequent sections of this manual will show, it requires community-wide involvement, focused catechetical efforts, and engaging ritual celebrations to create the kind of atmosphere and to support experiences powerful enough to reach the elect on a deep, transformative level. The season cannot be "business as usual" in the parish, and the catechumenal team will need to provide creative leadership in order to put in place the structures and to reinforce attitudes consistent with the new vision called for in the Rite. Particularly at this point in history, when the majority of Catholics still operate out of a pre–Vatican II mind-set in regard to the nature of Lent, there will need to be carefully planned and patiently executed efforts for many years if a baptismal spirituality is to be rooted deeply in people's experience of Lent as the time of purification and enlightenment in preparation for the Sacraments of Initiation.

The very name, Period of Purification and Enlightenment, indicates something of the balanced approach called for in the Rite. Centuries of tradition have already convinced us that Lent is a time of purification—little need to reinforce that awareness. Enlightenment, however, is a new (but truly ancient) notion in the Lenten context for most Catholics. In fact, in the early centuries of the Church the baptized were often referred to as the "enlightened" ones. Today, this term needs to form new associations with the initiatory process in the minds of every Catholic. The Church must recapture the dynamic, baptismal images associated with enlightenment that are available in the Scriptures and in the early tradition. The Johannine theme of light, especially as proclaimed in the scrutiny gospel of the man born blind (as well as the same imagery used in various Pauline passages), will be invaluable for use in this long-term project of catechesis. Preaching and teaching about Christian initiation as enlightenment must occupy a good deal of attention for generations to come if the Church is to achieve the balanced understanding of this period called for by the name given to it in the Rite.

Perhaps the most valuable resources in this effort will be found in the prayers and rituals contained in the Rite itself. The Rite of Election (and, in the dioceses of the United States, the parish-based Rite of Sending) is a wonderful proclamation of God's activity in the life of the elect. The emphasis is on God's grace which calls, chooses, and enlightens—not on any achievement of the elect accomplished through penitential disciplines or other efforts of their own. In a similar vein, the presentations are eloquent forms of ritual catechesis, aimed at enlightening the elect by formally handing over to them two precious carriers of Christian faith, the Creed and the Our Father. Though clearly to be taken in a symbolic rather than a literal sense, these ritual

---

Where to Go in the RCIA (USA Edition) for a Deeper Understanding

Nature of the Period
#7.3, 8, 138–40

Proper or Usual Times
#19–21, 26, 29–30, 104–05

Rite of Sending
#106–17

Rite of Election
#118–137

Scrutinies
#141–146, 150–56, 164–77

Presentations
#147–49, 157–63, 178–84

gestures do reinforce the idea that the Church opens up the mind and heart of the elect by sharing with them the treasures of faith. "The Creed, as it recalls the wonderful deeds of God for the salvation of the human race, suffuses the vision of the elect with the sure light of faith. The Lord's Prayer fills them with a deeper realization of the new spirit of adoption by which they will call God their Father, especially in the midst of the eucharistic assembly" (RCIA, 147). Enlightenment happens at the hands of the Church, indeed, in the midst of the Church, and is not the product of solitary research or effort on the part of the elect.

Even the Scrutinies, which because of their exorcistic focus could easily seem to be solely about purification, are described in the Rite as being "meant to uncover, then heal all that is weak, defective, or sinful in the hearts of the elect; to bring out, then strengthen all that is upright, strong, and good" (RCIA, 141). These rituals help the elect to achieve "an intimate knowledge of Christ and his Church" (RCIA, 142). By them the elect "are instructed gradually about the mystery of sin . . . [and] their spirit is filled with Christ the Redeemer" (RCIA, 143).

It is worth noting that the Rite (RCIA, 146) as well as the Roman *Lectionary* (Introduction, 13.1) encourages the use of Year A readings on the Third, Fourth, and Fifth Sunday of Lent, especially when the Scrutinies are celebrated with the elect. The imagery of the prayers used in the Scrutinies has been carefully chosen to echo the major themes of the Year A gospel readings (light, water, and resurrection). The three Johannine gospel readings now found in Year A are among the Church's most ancient catechetical texts associated with baptism. In the early Church, when Lent lasted only three weeks, these were the gospel readings used on those Sundays to prepare the catechumens for their Easter initiation. Parishes today that use the readings of Year B or Year C in place of those for Year A fail to appreciate how integral to baptism are the three great readings from the Gospel of John. The value of the Johannine texts is so great that their use even every year seems appropriate.

The final rites of the Period of Purification and Enlightenment are the so-called Preparation Rites on Holy Saturday. When the presentation of the Creed has been done earlier, the recitation of the Creed by the elect on Holy Saturday morning is meant to testify to their complete assimilation of the faith, the enlightenment that has taken place in the course of the forty days.

Chapter 2
The Elect and the Candidates

*H*aving looked at the history and structure of this period, it is appropriate now to turn to the people who are at the center of the movement of this season of purification and enlightenment: the elect and the baptized candidates who will complete their initiation at Easter.

Discernment for Election

Who are the elect? As Lent approaches, the Church endeavors to discover who among the catechumens will be ready to become the elect. A careful discernment takes place at this time to determine who will be the elect. Questions are raised and weighed carefully for each person in the process: Has the work of the catechumenate period (RCIA, 75) been undertaken sufficiently in this person's life? Have the dispositions shown at the Rite of Acceptance—the desire to seek Christ and learn to live as members of the Christian community—come to a new level of maturity such that the desire for the sacraments, indeed for union with Christ, is well founded?

The sufficient progress in faith of each individual is not taken for granted but is a question to be considered with prudence. It is, after all, a matter of great importance. If conversion has not grown and deepened, there is a real danger that the holy commitment of baptism will be entered into prematurely. Such premature commitments, like the marriage of adolescents, are all too easily broken—not through insincerity or bad will on anyone's part, but simply because the basis for these commitments is too shallow. Respect for the sacraments and respect for the needs of individuals demand discernment on the part of the Church.

From its earliest history, Christian initiation in the catechumenate has included a discernment before the Rite of Election. Before the sacraments can be celebrated, the Church must ask: Is this person ready to enter into this most sacred covenant?

The "Easter Bypass"

Because initiation can take several years to complete and the catechumenate period alone normally lasts a full year (see *National Statutes*, 6), there will be some catechumens who do not become elect this year and some candidates for whom this will not be their period of purification and enlightenment. This is not a negative reflection on them or a sign that something is lacking in the process. Rather, it is a sign of respect for the fact that each person is different and must take the time necessary for conversion to deepen and mature.

These catechumens and candidates journey through Lent while still in the catechumenate period. They are dismissed with those undergoing purification and enlightenment after the Liturgy of the Word at Sunday Mass as usual, but they are not the focus of the community's prayer in the rituals of purification and enlightenment, such as the Rite of Election and the Scrutinies. They do not receive the sacraments at Easter. Their agenda remains as it is described in paragraph 75 of the ritual text, and they look forward to entering the Period of Purification and Enlightenment at some later time.

Those baptized candidates who are following the whole process of formation that the catechumenate offers likewise find this a time for discernment. Has their formation progressed far enough at this point that the celebration of the sacraments can take place at Easter with integrity? Or is more time needed for their faith and the dispositions they manifested at the Rite of Welcome to become mature?

For some who have only been in the process a short time it will be clear that they are not yet ready to become the elect. For others, the ingredients of conversion may be present in them, but in sifting through their experience they and the community discover that the mix needs to "cook more"; the time is not yet right. By patiently and respectfully attending to the movements of the Spirit in each person's life, the Church comes to an awareness of the right time for that person to move into the next stage of the process.

Recognizing signs that the time is right for someone to pass from the catechumenate period into the Period of Purification and Enlightenment is a task that requires prayerful care and attention. The *Rite of Christian Initiation of Adults* gives the Church guidance in this.

Some of the things the Rite asks that the Church look for in those about to become the elect are found in paragraph 120. The Rite speaks of:

✧ Signs of change
". . . the catechumens are expected to have undergone a *conversion in mind and in action* . . ." (author's emphasis)
(I think and act differently because of my growing relationship with God, Christ, and the Church.)

✧ Appropriate knowledge
". . . to have developed a *sufficient acquaintance with Christian teaching. . . .*" (author's emphasis)
(I have a good grasp of Christian teaching, even though I may still have questions.)

✧ Qualities of life
". . . as well as a *spirit of faith and charity.*" (author's emphasis)
(There is evidence in my life of trust in God; love for God and neighbor motivates me.)

✧ Appropriate desire for the sacraments
"With *deliberate will and an enlightened faith* they must have the *intention* to receive the sacraments of the Church . . ." (author's emphasis)
(I am not merely carried along by the desire of others nor am I motivated by false or superstitious expectations of what the sacraments will do for me. Rather, I myself truly desire the sacraments and want them in an appropriate way.)

In the Rite of Election itself (RCIA, 131B), the godparents are asked to give witness to the sufficient readiness of the catechumens who are presented for election. The questions the godparents are asked point to some of the signs that these catechumens are ready to become the elect. The qualities mentioned are indeed simple and ordinary. Yet at their heart these simple actions are a profound witness to a growing relationship with Christ and with the Church:

- ❖ They have listened to the Word of God proclaimed by the Church.

- ❖ They have responded to that Word and begun to walk in God's presence.

- ❖ They have shared the company of their Christian brothers and sisters and joined with them in prayer.

These qualities are is further spelled out in these paragraphs of the Rite, which describe the agenda of the catechumenate period:

- ❖ Attentive listening to the Word is not only expressed by attendance at the Liturgy of the Word at Sunday Mass or by participation in catechetical sessions, but also is seen in a growing awareness of the mystery of salvation (75.1) and in how the Word nurtures a relationship with God and a life of faith (78).

- ❖ Responding to the Word and walking in God's presence includes bearing "witness to the faith" (75.2), practicing love of neighbor "even at the cost of self-renunciation" (75.2), and engaging in acts of apostolic service (75.4).

- ❖ Sharing in the company of Christians is not merely taking part in a social circle. Christian community provides the loving bond that sustains the newly converted in the midst of "divisions and separations" that are the cost of faith (75.2). Sharing in the company of Christians also means belonging to a faith family with whom one shares "the joy that God gives without measure" (75.2). It includes the prayer that is proper to the liturgical rites of the Church (75.3) as well as spontaneous moments of prayer shared as occasions arise.

As Lent draws near, the catechumenate director organizes the discernment process. The form the discernment will take can vary, depending on the parish and the people. The catechumens and candidates with their sponsors, possible godparents, and others on the team—including clergy, catechists, and so on— might be asked to reflect on the progress in faith that each catechumen and candidate has made. Individual conversations with each catechumen or candidate are necessary to the process. The sponsors' contribution to the discernment is especially important. It may be elicited by having the sponsors participate in the same conversation with the catechumen, by gathering all the sponsors as a group, or again by providing opportunities to talk one-to-one. Catechists also may have keen and helpful insights. The other catechumens and candidates may be consulted. Some parishes even have a discernment day, during which such reflections can be shared and meditated upon. Whichever of these strategies are pursued, they should be permeated by a spirit of prayer and respectful listening. Finally, everyone should learn the results of the discernment in ample time to prepare for the Rite of Sending and Rite of Election.

Celebrating the Rite of Election

At the Rite of Election there is much to celebrate. It gathers up, in symbolic fashion, all that has come before it in the previous period and launches the elect and the community into what lies ahead. In the Rite of Election, the bishop invites the godparents to witness to the catechumens' readiness and asks the catechumens themselves to declare their assent and to inscribe their names in the Book of the Elect. Although the ritual gestures of testimony and signing (or presenting the names for enrollment, if they were signed earlier) symbolize commitment, the entire celebration rests on a deeper foundation: the realization that it is God's action, God's choosing, and God's grace which have brought these catechumens to this threshold moment in their conversion. When the bishop declares them to be elect, he does so in the name of God, on whose behalf the Church acts (RCIA, 119).

The Christian life is full of paradox: Those who lose themselves find themselves, the last will be first, those who humble themselves will be exalted, the poor are blessed. In the Rite of Election, the Church celebrates yet another paradox. The effort, striving, and devotion of conversion is celebrated as God's gift. The evidence of conversion that we bring to God simply returns that which God has given to us first. Human merit rests on divine grace. "It was not you who chose me, but I who chose you and appointed you to go and bear fruit that will remain." (John 15:16, NAB).

The grandeur of the celebration of election—which takes place in the assembly of the whole local church, with the bishop presiding—can be a sign to the elect that the great work of God's salvation and mission, in which they are called to participate, indeed always exceeds our expectations.

Celebrating the Rites Belonging to the Period of Purification and Enlightenment

THE SCRUTINIES

Election is a joyful celebration, but it also has a certain solemnity, because it begins the serious business of the Lenten season of purification and enlightenment. Lent carries through the implications of the decision made in election—the decision to approach font and table, to die and rise with the Lord, to drink from the cup that Jesus drank. Throughout the Lenten season the elect are at the center of the parish community's prayer as they "wrestle with demons" and as "angels wait on them." Their catechesis during this period must allow ample time for reflection on the experience of the Scrutinies. What is stirring in the elect as they hear the Scriptures and prayers of these powerful rites? What do they experience as they kneel on the floor and as hands are laid on them? To what new place of vulnerability, healing, and freedom do they feel called by the Spirit in these rites?

In the Scrutinies on the Third, Fourth, and Fifth Sunday of Lent, the elect are prayed for under the banner of the gospels of Year A. The powerful symbols of water, light, and life, which are central to the baptismal rites, are opened up by these readings and the rituals constructed around them. In the reflections on the Scrutinies, the elect themselves fill each of these symbols with specific content. As they reflect on their own lives and the state of the world in which they live, water and thirst, light and blindness, and life and death easily gain shape, texture, color, faces, and names. As the Scrutinies progress, the elect learn that some of these faces and names are indeed our own.

The Scrutinies are more than an exercise in awareness of personal sin; they are a faith-filled grappling with a world in which sin reigns. The Church does not pray in the Scrutinies merely for moral improvement but rather for liberation from the sin that is entrenched in the human condition itself. With each successive Scrutiny the elect are expected to progress in their understanding of sin and their own profound awareness that Christ is the Redeemer of the world. A purely personal insight ("Jesus is my Savior"), powerful though it may be, is not enough. The elect must hear Jesus proclaim himself to be the people's long-awaited Messiah (Samaritan woman), the apocalyptic Son of Man (man born blind), the resurrection and the life (raising of Lazarus), and must understand that Christ is truly the Savior of the world.

THE PRESENTATIONS

During the week following the first Scrutiny, the elect are presented with the Creed, and during the week following the third Scrutiny they are presented with the Lord's Prayer. These two treasures of the Tradition, which are passed on ritually by the community of faith, may not be objectively new or hitherto unknown to the elect. The point of presenting them is, rather, that they will belong to the elect in a new way because of having been presented to them. Having received them formally and publicly from the community of faith at a time near to the Easter mysteries, the elect are encouraged to appreciate the centrality of the Creed and the Lord's Prayer among all the texts of our Tradition, and they learn the importance they must attach to holding fast to them in their own lives. The Creed and Lord's Prayer become a sacred trust once they are formally entrusted to them by the Church.

For pastoral reasons these two presentations may be cele-brated earlier, during the catechumenate period, rather than at this time.

THE PREPARATION RITES

Holy Saturday is intended as a time of prayer and fasting for the elect and the candidates who will receive sacraments at the Easter Vigil. It is important that they refrain from work and spend time in reflection and prayer. The elect and candidates do not participate in a rehearsal for the ritual of the Easter Vigil, although they will need to be instructed about practical details, such as what to wear. Their experience of the events of Holy Saturday night is best kept for the event itself, with the godpar-ents and sponsors as guides.

One of the ways in which the whole of Holy Saturday is kept sacred is by the preparation rites that occur sometime during the day. A wide variety of possible rites are available for this time such as the ephpheta, the recitation of the Creed, the presentation of the Lord's Prayer, or the giving of a new name, if these have not been celebrated earlier. All of these possibilities concern actions that will take place later, in the Vigil, and so truly are a preparation for what is coming. Whichever rites are chosen, their celebration in a simple fashion underlines the prayerful nature of the day.

The Baptized Candidates

The baptized candidates, like the elect, are on a journey that will ultimately lead them to full participation in the Eucharist. Unlike the elect, however, the conversion of the candidates is based on the baptism they have already received, the full effects of which they are striving to develop. So while they too undergo a period of purification and enlightenment along with the elect—and at times we recognize and pray for them in special ways—the baptized candidates nevertheless are different from the elect. In the rituals of this period, and some of the pastoral strategies proper to this period, we find the difference expressed.

Ritual Distinctions

Because our rituals proclaim who we are, we must take care in how we use them with the baptized candidates. It would be easy to mix everyone together indiscriminately, because all are on a faith journey. But instead we are called upon to keep clear distinctions between these two groups. In the Period of Purification and Enlightenment, when so much ritual activity gives shape to the season, observing these distinctions becomes particularly notable and valuable. When distinctions between the baptized candidates and the elect are kept, three goals are served:

First, the community is helped to appreciate more clearly the awesome mystery of baptism. The rites for the elect make clear that *the journey of the elect is pivotal,* because through the sacrament of Baptism in its fullness, the elect will become a new creation. The journey of the unbaptized is the most fundamental of all of our rites of passage and deserves attention. Far from causing the rest of the faithful to be distanced from the elect, the baptismal focus of the rites for the elect is intended to draw us into a deeper identification with them. We all experience anew something of our own baptism when we attend to the movement of the elect through this season.

Second, when appropriate ritual distinctions are kept, we become more aware of how the baptized candidates are already *one with the faithful* because of their baptism. The Lenten journey of the baptized candidates, though still a focus of special pastoral care on the part of the Church, has much in common with the Lenten renewal of the faithful accomplished through prayer, works of charity, and celebration of the sacrament of Penance.

Third, by keeping careful distinctions between the baptized and the unbaptized, we honor *ecumenical sensitivities*. The way in which we treat non-Catholic candidates teaches our own community that we respect Christians from other churches. If we treat them as though they are not Christians, we have failed fundamentally to honor our Church's ecumenical commitment. Also, if we treat those candidates who were baptized in the Catholic Church as if they were unbaptized, we are saying implicitly that their baptism does not count.

The following summary presents at a glance the ritual distinctions between the elect and the candidates found in the U.S. edition of the Rite.

◇ In the *Rite of Election and Call to Continuing Conversion* (USA, 547ff.), the baptized candidates do not sign the Book of the Elect. They, like the faithful, are already, figuratively speaking, "enrolled" because of their baptism. Nevertheless, they have a place in this Rite. The beginning of the Period of Purification and Enlightenment is marked ritually for the baptized candidates by the calling of their names, by the testimony of their sponsors, and by the bishop recognizing their progress and enjoining them to "be faithful to [their] baptismal covenant."

◇ Those who during the catechumenate period were called catechumens experience a change of status because of their participation in the Rite of Election. They are no longer called "catechumens," but are called the "elect." The baptized candidates, on the other hand, remain what they were before. We do not refer to them as the elect, but simply continue to call them "candidates."

Different Nations, Different Norms

Some episcopal conferences have no particular rites for the baptized candidates. Canada has developed separate rites for them that are not to be combined with the rites for the unbaptized, except in the case of the Easter Vigil.

In the dioceses of the United States, both combined rites (for the baptized and the unbaptized) and separate rites have been written, and guidance in using them has been given in the *National Statutes*. Where reference is made to parts of the ritual text that are special to the United States, the designation USA and the paragraph number is given.

✧ Unlike the elect, who from the Rite of Election onward are accompanied by a godparent, the baptized candidates continue in this period to journey with their sponsors who have accompanied them since the earlier stages of the process.

✧ During the Scrutinies, the candidates participate in praying for the elect as the faithful do. They themselves are not the special focus of the community's prayer in the Scrutinies. Indeed, the scrutiny prayers preserve a strong baptismal flavor, which marks them as prayers for the elect alone. For the candidates, a *penitential rite* —similar to a Scrutiny but with language crafted for the baptized candidates—may be celebrated on the Second Sunday of Lent or some other time when the community gathers (USA, 462).

✧ The baptized candidates may celebrate the sacrament of Penance during this time, but the elect do not. For many candidates, this will be their first experience of this sacrament of forgiveness and healing. In the edition of the Rite written for the dioceses of Canada, encouragement is given for the candidates to receive a lighted baptismal candle at the conclusion of a communal celebration of the sacrament of Penance to show the connection of this sacrament to the renewal of baptism (Canada, 530).

✧ The Catholic Church never baptizes anyone who is already validly baptized. At the Easter Vigil, the baptized candidates renew their baptismal promises with the assembly, celebrate the Rite of Reception if they were baptized in a non-Catholic church, are confirmed (if they are not already validly confirmed), and join us in eucharistic communion. The confirmation of anyone received into the full communion of the Catholic Church may not be delayed to another time. Permission to confirm Catholics who are completing their Christian initiation should be obtained from the local Ordinary.

Pastoral Strategies

BEFORE THE PERIOD OF PURIFICATION AND ENLIGHTENMENT

Often the baptized candidates arrive in the initiation process with little awareness of the value of their baptism. Part of the ministry of the Church to these candidates is to gradually, through catechesis and ritual, bring them to a consciousness of the gift they possess in their baptism. The time to begin helping the baptized candidates develop a respect for their own baptism is early in the process. Beginning in the precatechumenate and continuing throughout the catechumenate period, there are many occasions to reflect on and affirm their baptism. By the time we reach the Period of Purification and Enlightenment, we should already have helped the candidates to develop a positive awareness of the baptism they have already received. Some ways we can do this are:

✧ Having the baptized candidates get in touch with the event of their baptism through stories, photographs, and members of their family who may remember it.

✧ Praying with them and for them in a way that recalls the gift of their baptism.

✧ Being clear about what the Church teaches, namely, that baptism is a covenant to which God remains faithful, even if we have not been aware of it or responded until now.

✧ Reminding the candidates that when they take part in the mission of the Church through works of justice, mercy, and love, they are living out the promise of their baptism.

If this groundwork has been laid in the earlier stages of the process, the Period of Purification and Enlightenment will not be a time when the baptized candidates feel "left out" and wish they could be baptized all over again. Rather, they will be aware of the goodness of their own identity and of the necessity and importance of ongoing conversion for living the Christian life.

DURING THE PERIOD OF PURIFICATION AND ENLIGHTENMENT

The baptized candidates participate in the reflections on the Lenten Scriptures with the elect and share in all the spiritual preparations for and reflections on the Scrutinies and the Penitential Rite. In addition, they may have the Creed and the Lord's Prayer presented to them if they entered the process as uncatechized adults (RCIA, 407). Even if there are no elect in the parish in a given year, the candidates nevertheless are called to undertake with the whole Church the spiritual tasks of coming to a deeper awareness of both "the mystery of sin, from which the whole world and every person longs to be delivered," and the mystery of Christ the Redeemer, who fills the spirit of the believer with living water, light, and life (RCIA, 143). By sustained, prayerful reflection on the gospel readings of this season, the candidates are prepared for Easter. Participation with the community of faith in the common Lenten disciplines of prayer, fasting, and almsgiving is also important for the candidates. The deepening spiritual awareness cultivated by the initiation process is not divorced from life but engages all of life, especially their experience of doing the works of justice and mercy that was so great a part of their formation in the catechumenate period.

Rite of Reception Outside the Easter Vigil

Some candidates for reception into the full communion of the Catholic Church have a mature Christian commitment and have been living their faith for a long time. These individuals are far different from the catechumens and uncatechized candidates, who are unchurched and have little faith experience. Consequently, they do not need the full program of formation that the catechumenate period offers, although a certain time of preparation is altogether appropriate. Such individuals may be received into the Church at a Sunday liturgy, usually during Ordinary Time (*National Statutes,* 32). Preaching at such a celebration offers a wonderful occasion to speak about Christian Unity—a goal to which the Catholic Church is deeply committed. The readings and texts from the Mass "For the Unity of Christians" may be used at such a celebration as well (RCIA, 487).

Offering the candidates an opportunity to participate in the sacrament of Penance during this season is also valuable, though the timing of its celebration need not affect the rest of the process. When choosing occasions to invite the candidates to the sacrament, it is best to offer opportunities when they will not feel coerced. Because of the communal nature of the entire process, many parishes introduce the candidates to this sacrament through a parish communal celebration with individual confessions. Some parishes may make the opportunity for confession available during a retreat, for those who wish to participate. And in some situations, individual appointments are made with a priest. Whatever the setting, some time should be set aside for the immediate preparation for this event.

PREPARATION FOR THE SACRAMENT OF PENANCE

Several times over the course of each liturgical year, the Sunday readings offer opportunities to catechize on sin, God's forgiveness, our Catholic understanding of sacrament in general, and the sacrament of Penance in particular. For example, the following Sundays in Year C lend themselves to such catechesis: the Third Sunday of Advent; the Third, Fourth, and Fifth Sunday of Lent; and the Eighth, Eleventh, Fifteenth, Eighteenth, Twentieth, and Twenty-fourth Sunday in Ordinary Time. Year A and Year B afford many similar opportunities.

The formation of conscience is a concern throughout the catechumenate, and candidates will have learned ways to examine their conscience throughout the process. Questions and concerns about the practice of confessing one's sins will be brought to the surface on these occasions and should not be deferred until the Period of Purification and Enlightenment.

During the Period of the Catechumenate, therefore, most of the long-range preparation for the sacrament of Penance will have taken place. What remains is the immediate preparation—which is simple and ought not to be belabored—and the celebration of the sacrament itself. Immediate preparation would include:

> ✧ *Review of the form of the celebration*
> The candidates should be familiar with the outline of the communal rite or individual rite and understand what they are to do in it (see Handout 23). It is helpful if the confessor(s) can meet with the candidates and speak to them during this time to establish a comfortable relationship with them. If they chose to go to a confessor who does not know them, they should tell the confessor that they are candidates and that this is their first celebration of the sacrament. Assure them that the priest confessor is there to minster to them and will help them.

❖ *Prayerful examination of conscience*

When looking over a lifetime, it may seem daunting to try to recall and confess all of one's sins. It is important that the candidates not become overwhelmed with detail but rather are able to identify any serious sinful deeds or patterns of the past and present that need forgiveness. Using one of the examinations of conscience from the Rite of Penance (see Handout 24), a catechist or confessor, in preparation for the Sacrament, may lead a group of candidates through a reflection on their lives. (Note: The parish communal celebration of penance may offer, within the celebration itself, both the time for and guidance in examining one's conscience which will make this step unnecessary.)

An examination of conscience is a deeply personal affair but the candidate need not experience it in isolation. The presence of the sponsor, as a fellow penitent and as someone available for conversation and questions, can support the candidate. It is important that the sponsors work out of an adult, post-Vatican II understanding of the sacrament in order to fulfill this role in a helpful way.

❖ *Time for questions*

Often we are not aware of the anxieties and concerns that may trouble an individual candidate while preparing for this sacrament. It is important to create an unhurried atmosphere in which any questions and concerns may be shared.

Sponsors and Godparents

Often the same person who was the sponsor for a catechumen becomes that person's godparent, although a different person may be chosen (RCIA, 10). The role of godparent begins before election. Indeed, the godparent is expected to take part in the discernment for election. The public role of the godparent begins at the Rite of Election and continues on throughout life (RCIA, 11).

The choice of a person for godparent needs to take into account the nature of the ministry. Being a godparent of an adult is not merely an honorific role that can be fulfilled by being present at the ritual of baptism. The ministry of the godparent continues the work of the sponsor in supporting and guiding the elect during the intense time of the Lenten forty-day retreat, during mystagogy, and beyond. Godparents must know their catechumens well enough to bear witness for them at the Rite of Election, as must the sponsors of candidates. Willingness to speak publicly on their behalf is important. In the case of the godparent, a lifelong relationship after baptism is envisioned as well. Godparents and sacramental sponsors of adults are subject to the same canonical requirements as godparents and sacramental sponsors of children: they must be fully initiated Catholics who live a life of faith and can set a good example.

If a person different from the sponsor is chosen to be godparent, the godparent ought to begin to participate in the process at once, sharing in the preparation for the Scrutinies and in other events such as, the presentations and any retreat days that are offered. The sponsor may continue to participate in these events as well, although the special role of the godparent takes precedence in the rites themselves.

For the baptized candidates, the sponsors who began with them in the catechumenate period will continue throughout the process. They too will participate in the preparations for the Scrutinies, the Presentations, retreat days, and so on.

Both the godparents of the elect and the sponsors of the baptized candidates also rehearse for the rituals themselves. The elect and the candidates do not rehearse. The role of the elect and candidates is to be fully attentive to whatever is happening in the rite at the "present" moment—free to forget about what will happen next, where they will stand, and so on. All of the practical matters of the celebration will be taken care of by the sponsors or godparents. They will also help to accommodate any special needs of the elect and candidates, such as an inability to kneel for the Scrutinies. They must be willing to prepare in order to guide their charges through the rituals with confidence.

The godparents, though chosen by the elect, must be approved by the priest (usually the pastor), and it is desirable that they be approved by the community as well. In actual practice, the approval of the community is usually represented by the catechumenate team, who would have a sense of who is appropriate.

Chapter 3
The Parish

*I*n the context of the parish, what takes place in the Period of Purification and Enlightenment is particularly important. Baptism is the central focus of *both* the parish celebration of Lent and of the Period of Purification and Enlightenment for the elect. While the elect are preparing for baptism, the entire community is preparing to renew their baptismal commitment at Easter. Just as the elect turn over to the power of Christ any hold that evil has on them, so too the community of the baptized once again turns over to Christ the ways of evil that lure them away from God. The elect come to know intimately Christ the Savior, who is the living water, the light of the world, and the resurrection and the life. At the same time the baptized renew their intimate relationship with Christ.

The *Rite of Christian Initiation of Adults* states explicitly that the elect and the entire community engage together in this period of spiritual preparation, which is centered on dying and rising with Christ in baptism (RCIA, 138). Moreover, the journey of the community and that of the elect do not merely take place next to each other. Rather, the purification and enlightenment experience of the elect—particularly in the celebration of the Scrutinies— provides a liturgical experience that acts as a catalyst for the community's own continuing conversion. The elect actually propel forward the community's baptismal renewal. And the community in turn, both by ministering to the elect and by earnestly undertaking its own renewal, supports and encourages the elect on their way to the Easter sacraments.

In order to implement the Church's vision of Lent, parish communities initially must take time to share this vision and talk together about it. Then they must determine what activities are and are not appropriate to help the community deepen their baptismal relationship with Christ. To start, the parish staff (preferably with some members of the community) may gather in a prayerful setting to talk about what Lent is. Those who will be involved in

The Vision of Lent

The vision of Lent as a preparation for or renewal of baptismal life in Christ sets the direction for the life of the entire parish during this season. During Lent all aspects of parish life—what happens and what does not happen—are determined by this baptismal focus. When Lent is lived in this way, parish staff members and parishioners continually comment on how their parishes become more alive spiritually and give more attention to justice concerns.

this conversation should read Chapter 1 and Chapter 2 of this manual in preparation for that discussion. Then, when gathered, they might consider these questions:

- ✧ What will help our parish experience Lent as a time of retreat, of spiritual recollection?
- ✧ What will help us live our lives more in harmony with Christ and the gospel message?
- ✧ What will enable us to see the connection between the conversion happening in those being initiated and in our own lives?

After prayer and shared reflection on the baptismal focus of Lent, the group may turn to particular aspects of parish life. Two possible questions for consideration are:

- ✧ What activities will take us away or sidetrack our parish from renewing our baptismal identity?
- ✧ What activities will better serve our parish's celebration of Lent if they occur at another time of the year?

Then the group may consider specific practices in the parish and talk about how the baptismal focus of Lent affects each one.

CELEBRATION OF INFANT BAPTISM

The Easter season is the proper time for celebrating baptism. In the celebration of infant baptism, the community present renews their baptismal promises. Lent is a time of preparation for the renewal of baptismal promises that takes place at the Easter celebrations. Unless an urgent need exists, infant baptisms may more appropriately be celebrated at one of the Sunday Masses of Easter.

CELEBRATION OF THE RITE OF MARRIAGE

The "Introduction" to the Rite of Marriage (11) indicates that when celebrating this sacrament during the seasons of Advent or Lent, the nature of these seasons should be taken into consideration. Because these seasons are not compatible with the festive aspect of most weddings, many parishes do not schedule weddings during Advent or Lent. In fact, some dioceses discourage weddings in Lent as a matter of policy. Because Lent is a penitential season, if the Rite of Marriage is celebrated, it should be done in a more simple fashion. It should be pointed out to engaged couples that purple cloths are used to decorate the worship space during Lent.

BUSINESS MEETINGS

Lent is a time of retreat and of spiritual recollection. A retreat is a time away from usual business to reflect, to take stock, to gain perspective, to pray. Some parishes do not have any business meetings during Lent. Groups such as the parish council, education commission, and finance committee gather instead for a time of prayer and faith sharing. Or, they simply do not meet and their individual members participate in other parish spiritual opportunities.

A RETREAT ENVIRONMENT

The Lenten retreat must have an appropriate environment. Consider various ways of encouraging a reflective environment when people come together for worship, small group faith sharing, or any other parish Lenten activity. The gospel reading proclaimed on the First Sunday of Lent states that Jesus was in the desert for forty days. For the forty days of Lent the Church also, symbolically, enters the desert for its annual retreat. "The desert" suggests a wilderness, a place of emptiness, stillness, and quiet without a lot of activity. It is in this quiet place away from daily noise and activity that God's voice can be heard and discernment of spirits occurs. Creating a desert landscape with rocks, sand, and cactus in every parish is not the intention. Rather, the desired simplicity, quiet, and stillness of the desert may be created environmentally in both worship and meeting spaces by removing clutter and by using simple purple cloths, a lighted candle, incense, and so on. Quiet, reflective music might be played at times when people gather for sharing. Hymns and prayer at the beginning of each gathering set a retreat tone.

PARISH STAFF RETREAT

The parish staff often works harder than ever during the time of Lent. While inviting the parish community to spend more time in prayer and reflection, the parish staff often does not heed its own suggestion. The parish leadership needs to find ways to retreat as well. A day or an overnight stay away to pray together without being absorbed in ministry to others can provide spiritual renewal for the staff during this season. Praying at the beginning of the morning, just before lunch, or at the end of the day also provides a way for the staff to live Lent more contemplatively. Closing the parish office two or three times during Lent for a time of prayer not only gives the staff time for spiritual reflection, but also speaks loudly to the parish about the true meaning of Lent.

BRINGING THE COMMUNITY ABOARD

Before Lent begins take some time to help the parish understand the focus of the season of Lent. This may be done through the homily, announcements at the Sunday Masses, bulletins and news-letters, a letter sent to parishioners, religious formation classes, and talking with various parish groups at their meetings. Using many forms of communication helps to reach a variety of people.

Provide a concrete, tangible tool to help the community focus on their own renewal of baptismal promises and conversion along with those preparing for initiation. For example, use questions like the following for the entire parish to consider during Lent to bring them to an awareness of their baptismal identity, conversion, and relationship with those being initiated:

⬧ What connection does the dying and rising of Jesus Christ have to our daily lives?

⬧ How does the spiritual journey of those preparing for initiation call our entire community to conversion?

These questions—or whatever touchstone is used—need to be placed before the community in an ongoing way. Initially they may be sent in a letter by the parish staff to all members of the parish. One parish prints the questions on a bookmark with the names of those to be initiated at the Vigil written on one side and a request for prayers for them on the other side. Keeping this focus also needs to be achieved through homilies, religious formation sessions, and various parish meetings.

Invite members of the parish to share their Lenten journey with others. The Catholic Church is a community; therefore, faith is not simply an individual experience. Encourage everyone in the parish to be connected with a small group and/or a faith companion during the Lenten season. Use existing small faith communities. Set up intergenerational groups, particularly involving families of those preparing for First Communion or Confirmation and those families who have recently had an infant baptized. Invite all families to participate in these groups. Folks already in the initiation process may continue in their own grouping or participate in other parish groupings. Parishes may choose to have existing groups such as the choir, St. Vincent de Paul Society, or parish council journey through Lent together. Within these groups, people may also have an individual companion with whom to share the Lenten journey.

These small groups can come together to talk about the questions listed above, to reflect on the Sunday Scripture readings to prepare for a Scrutiny (see "A Parish Mission"), for an evening or day of retreat, for evening prayer, and/or the communal celebration of penance. Provide one suggestion for gathering each week so that the small groups gather weekly during Lent. Groups may begin during the week of Ash Wednesday to set their direction toward the renewal of their baptism. Individuals may share with the group at this initial session the specific ways they want to live this Lenten season to renew their baptism. Or each small group could decide upon a particular action they will engage in together. Companions may take some time for faith sharing during the weekly gathering or may meet at another time for a deeper sharing and to pray together.

A PARISH MISSION

Many parishes have a mission during the season of Lent. Care must be taken that the mission incorporates the vision of Lent as a time of renewal of baptismal life. The mission needs to be integrated with the initiatory and reconciling aspects of the Lenten period, such as the preparation and celebration of Scrutinies and the communal celebration of the sacrament of Penance.

Each parish must determine ways to involve as many members of the parish as possible in this Lenten retreat. Be creative. Keep the vision before you and brainstorm how this can work in your parish.

Opportunities for Prayer, Fasting, and Works of Charity

Within the broad framework of renewing the meaning of baptism, specific practices help people to attend to their spiritual journey. Catholic tradition suggests using prayer, fasting, and works of charity for this renewal. Works of charity include almsgiving, an important aspect of giving in our culture. As Lent begins, the practices of prayer, fasting, and almsgiving are proclaimed in Matthew 6:1–6, 16–18, the gospel on Ash Wednesday. Prayer, fasting, and works of charity provide parishioners with concrete means to deepen their baptismal commitment. These may be done individually, within families, or through broader parish offerings.

Prayer, fasting, and works of charity all have as their goal growing in our relationship with God and others. These practices are not ends in themselves. For example, not eating between meals may help someone become more aware of a hunger for God, which may result in spending more time with God in prayer. Or becoming aware of hunger may lead a person to feel connected with the hungry of the world and take action on their behalf. In each case, fasting has helped the person grow. If fasting, however, only serves to demonstrate personal strength to be able to keep such a fast, then fasting has not served its spiritual purpose.

Offering these and other appropriate suggestions of ways to engage in prayer, fasting, and works of charity enlarges the vision of how meaningful and personal these traditional spiritual practices might be. Provide a bulletin insert naming various possibilities for prayer, fasting, and works of charity on the Sunday before Ash Wednesday (see sidebar on this page). Place a commitment form at the bottom of the insert. Individuals or a family can then display this form in a prominent place at home. For example, the commitment form may be placed on a prayer table or on the refrigerator.

In addition to the practices of prayer, fasting, and works of charity that may be done privately or as a family, the parish may offer opportunities to do some of these things with others. Many of the practices named in your bulletin insert (see sidebar on this page) could be done with a companion or by a small group.

Inviting the Parish to Prayer, Fasting, and Almsgiving

A simple bulletin insert can help parishioners to enter into Lenten renewal with the catechumens and candidates. Your parish staff or members of the parish Lenten planning team may have additional suggestions to add to these ideas.

Prayer

- Read Scripture _____ minutes a day.
- Pray as a family before meals. Pray for one another's needs.
- Participate more fully in Sunday Mass.
- Continue to pray over the Scriptures proclaimed at Sunday Mass to enflesh the Word.
- Take time to listen to what God wants to say to you.
- Take a walk alone to quiet down and simply be in God's presence.
- Take time to appreciate God's goodness in nature and in people.
- Pray your favorite prayers, the rosary, or take part in the celebration of weekday Mass.
- Write a letter to God in your journal. Then let God "write" to you.
- Pray for _____ minutes when you get up or before you go to bed.

Fasting

- Fast from watching TV. Spend this time with family members.
- Fast from snacks. Send the money saved to help the poor.
- Fast from new clothes and other consumer items. Give the money saved to a shelter helping the homeless.
- Fast from a full meal as a family. Make a meal of soup once a week. Share the money saved with the poor.
- Fast from _____ to become more aware of God and others.
- Fast from gossip.

Works of charity

- Give of your time to become more aware of others.
- Write letters to relatives.
- Visit the elderly, people who are homebound or in a nursing home, or prisoners.
- Help out a brother or sister, neighbor or friend.
- Spend time with your family.
- Share your financial resources with those in need.
- Volunteer your time at a soup kitchen.
- Give your time to find out more about people in our world who have special needs such as, people in Third World countries, the homeless, persons with AIDS, and so on.
- Talk with someone toward whom you feel prejudiced.

The parish may combine two or more of these practices. For example, a simple soup supper may be combined with a speaker educating the parishioners about people living in the area who are hungry and poor and about the many possible ways of reaching out to them. The soup supper could be followed by a celebration of evening prayer or the Stations of the Cross. Members of the parish could serve food at a soup kitchen and come back to the parish for a time of reflection and prayer.

The Rite of Sending for Election

The Rite of Election, which generally coincides with the First Sunday of Lent, is celebrated with the bishop, usually at the cathedral; but the Rite of Sending for Election takes place beforehand in the midst of the parish community. Because the participation of the community is integral to the whole initiation process (RCIA, 9), the parish community participates in the discernment prior to this rite as well as in the celebration of the Rite of Sending for Election. A further look at these two moments of the initiation process will illustrate ways the community can participate.

Involving the community in the deliberation about the catechumens' readiness for the celebration of election demands that members of the parish community know the catechumens and candidates. This process begins long before the discernment for the Rite of Election. Parishioners come to know catechumens and candidates in various ways. Neighbors, coworkers, or those with children in the same class or on the same sports team can be informed about the person's participation in the catechumenate. The catechumens and candidates may be invited to participate in a small faith community or in some form of parish outreach. They can be welcomed to take part in various parish social activities. Individuals, families, a school class, or the homebound may be invited to pray for a particular catechumen or candidate. These prayer sponsors may get to know the catechumens and candidates by meeting them at various times. When the community knows the catechumens and candidates, a genuine sharing in discernment becomes possible (see sidebar on this page).

Signs of readiness for celebrating the Rite of Election can be elicited from members of the parish according to the way in which the discernment process occurs within the parish. The coordinator or a team member can personally talk with these parishioners, or the parishioners can be asked to write about their observations. (See *Discerning Disciples: Listening for God's Voice in Christian Initiation* by Donna Steffen, Paulist Press, 1997 for further suggestions about discernment processes.)

The Rite of Election celebrates that God has elected the catechumen for the Easter sacraments this year. Concrete signs of how God is acting in the catechumen are the focus of the input of the members of the parish community. What is sought after is not so much a statement of all the good things the person has

Sharing in Discernment

Several months before the Rite of Sending, names of individuals who know the various catechumens and candidates could be collected through a pulpit or bulletin announcement or from the catechumens and candidates themselves. Here is an example of a bulletin announcement:

We would like to thank you for your prayers for our catechumens and candidates. On March 7th some of our catechumens will begin preparation for baptism, and some of our candidates will begin preparation to complete their initiation or to be received into the full communion of the Catholic Church. Many of you know them personally. We ask two favors. First, continue to keep them in your prayers. Second, if you have a story of seeing faith alive in one of them that you think is appropriate to share, please call the initiation coordinator, (name of coordinator).

done, such as attending sessions or prayer experiences. Rather, what is hoped for are examples of the ways God is acting in and through the person. In what ways are gospel values, such as justice, forgiveness, and dependence on God shown through this catechumen? In what ways are the living of such values having an effect on the broader community? The same questions are relevant for the baptized candidates who are preparing to receive sacraments at Easter and will be sharing in the Period of Purification and Enlightenment with the elect.

Participating in this discernment process fosters in the parish community the understanding that it is the Church that is sharing in the responsibility and privilege of initiating new members. In discerning signs of God's election of others, the parish itself also experiences being challenged to live the Gospel more earnestly.

Taking part in discerning the readiness of catechumens for election also helps the parish become more involved in the celebration of the Rite of Sending. When catechumens and candidates are called forth and testimony is given about them, the members of the assembly who have given their input will know the significance of what is spoken. If members of the assembly are asked either for a communal affirmation or an individual statement of testimony, those who know the catechumens and candidates personally will be especially aware of the significance of the witness given. All present will be affected by this testimony.

The two primary ritual actions in the Rite of Sending are the giving of testimony and the signing of names in the Book of the Elect (if they are not to be signed in the Rite of Election itself). Only the catechumens enroll their names in the Book of the Elect, but their godparents, because of their role, may also sign the book along with the elect if this is the local custom. Those who have been baptized in another Christian faith tradition, or who were baptized in the Catholic Church and are completing their initiation, are already elect by means of their baptism. The candidates, therefore, do not sign the Book of the Elect.

The members of the parish community are already elect by means of their baptism. Stating in the Rite of Sending that baptized candidates do not enroll their names because they and the rest of the parish community are already elect by their baptism helps the entire community grasp in a new way the meaning of their baptism.

Having the candidates present a copy of their baptismal certificate at the Rite of Sending to the presider is an action that highlights the candidates' baptismal status that some parishes have adopted. This action would take place near the Book of the Elect as a sign to the community that in baptism we become God's elect.

The very manner in which the Rite of Sending is celebrated can do much to insure that the parish experiences itself as a faith-filled assembly actively engaged in the initiation process. This can be accomplished easily and powerfully by placing the catechumens in the midst of the assembly or in various places throughout the assembly for the giving of testimony by the godparents and sponsors. Using acclamations that are known and easy to sing and that fit the meaning of the rite will help the community actively participate in the ritual action. Proudly carrying the Book of the Elect throughout the assembly after the signing, while the community sings an acclamation, also demonstrates that the Church gathered is active in this ritual. The physical gesture of the entire assembly extending hands in prayer over the catechumens and candidates facilitates the community actively participating in celebrating this rite—as it is called to do.

Placing the Book of the Elect in the midst of the assembly for all the Masses on this Sunday, even those that precede the Rite of Sending, keeps this important moment before the entire parish community. Reference to the election that the community is celebrating also needs to be included in the homily and intercessions at all the parish Masses on this Sunday.

The Presentations

The presentations of the Creed and of the Lord's Prayer are intended to be celebrated within the community and not simply outside the assembly in a gathering of the elect with their godparents and the catechumenate team. The *Rite of Christian Initiation of Adults* presumes that the handing on of the Creed and of the Lord's Prayer takes place during Mass. People of God, represented by the local parish, are truly the vehicle for the handing on of the Church's tradition of faith and prayer that is symbolized by these presentations.

It is significant that the ritual text calls for the voice of the community of the faithful to be the medium for presenting the Creed. The Lord's Prayer too is presented in a verbal proclamation of the gospel text. Both presentations of these living symbols of the Faith have to take place within the gathered assembly. For the presentation of the Creed and of the Lord's Prayer, the presider might, therefore, invite the elect to stand in the midst of the assembly of the faithful The presider might also encourage the community to be conscious that they are handing on the Faith of the Church to these elect and to slowly and deliberately join in professing that faith as they pray the Creed together.

The Scrutinies

The Scrutinies for the elect are celebrated on the Third, Fourth, and Fifth Sunday of Lent. In order to make these Scrutinies as meaningful as possible, the elect take time to name the particular aspects of their life for which they desire freedom from the power of sin. The focus of this exercise is not so much to ask forgiveness or to set an agenda for moral improvement, but, by acknowledging a fundamental need for God, to experience the redemption that Christ offers. This preparation could occur at one gathering before the first Scrutiny, or it could take place before

each of the three Scrutinies, which would encourage the participants to deepen their awareness in each successive preparation.

The Scrutinies celebrate a deep mystery of our spiritual
journey. Through the Scrutinies the elect, in preparation for
baptism, are turning over to God any hold sin has on them.
Along with the elect, the entire church community is allowing
God's grace to scrutinize their hearts as they too once again and
more fully turn over to God any hold sin has on them. The elect
and the community of the faithful together come to know Christ,
who is a fountain of living water, the Light of the world, and
everlasting life. The elect are living symbols for the entire
community on their journey of renewing their own baptismal
commitment. It is very appropriate, then, for the parish members
to join with the elect both in the Scrutiny preparation as well as
in the celebrations of the Scrutinies themselves.

The assembly of the faithful may be invited to prepare for
the Scrutinies in various ways. They could participate in the
actual Scrutiny preparation sessions with the elect. (See pages
111–122 in this manual for sample preparation sessions.) Because
of the desire to involve as many members of the parish as
possible, Scrutiny preparation sessions could take place at several
times during the week preceding a Scrutiny. If members of the
parish are unable to participate in any of these sessions, they
may share with a companion how they are being invited to let
go of any sinful patterns or tendencies in their life. They may
also share the ways in which they are knowing and experiencing
Christ ever more deeply. The parish could provide a reflective
tool for this conversation, which includes prayer, a reading of at
least one of the Scriptures of the given Sunday, and questions for
reflection.

If the assembly has been involved in Scrutiny preparation,
the actual celebration of the Scrutinies will become even more
meaningful. To highlight the role of the community, the elect
may be situated in the midst of the assembly rather than in the
sanctuary. The community more fully participates in the intercessions when responses are sung and not simply recited.

Though the Scrutiny is often celebrated only during one celebration of Sunday Mass, the readings from Year A may be used at
all of the Masses on the Third, Fourth, and Fifth Sunday of Lent.
The intercessions from the Scrutiny may be incorporated in an
adapted form into the general intercessions. By using an appropriate invitation leading into these intercessions, the presider can
make the assembly more conscious that, as a crucial dimension
of its intercessory prayer during this season, the entire community is praying both for the elect as well as for its own
conversion.

The Sacrament of Penance

Sacraments celebrate the way God's grace is acting within a person and the community of the faithful. Before a person approaches the sacrament of Penance, or Reconciliation, the reality of reconciliation taking place within one's deepest self, with others, with creation, and with God has begun taking place.

The period in which the Scrutinies are celebrated is a particularly rich time of engaging this reconciling process. Participating in the Scrutiny preparation sessions, hearing the powerful scrutiny gospels proclaimed, and praying for the elect and the community present to be freed from sin and filled with Christ have the effect of moving the gathered Church toward conversion. The parish celebration of penance, then, is well placed after the last Scrutiny on the Fifth Sunday of Lent before the celebration of the Easter Triduum begins.

The preparation for and celebration of the Scrutinies focus on social and systemic sin as well as personal sin and patterns of sinfulness in individuals. Through the Scrutinies, the community comes to understand in a fuller way the social impact of sin. The celebration of the communal rite of reconciliation is an appropriate next step for the baptized community. With this broader awareness of sin, the community is able to pray for and with one another for a deep reconciliation. The baptized candidates may be encouraged to participate in this sacrament with the community. The experience of being personally forgiven along with the other members of the assembly is a very powerful experience. Especially in its communal form, the sacrament of Penance enables the community to experience itself as a Church being renewed, made new again.

With the awareness that the community is undergoing a renewal of its baptismal commitment, the Scripture readings chosen for this communal celebration of the sacrament may reflect this understanding. Scripture readings expressing baptismal imagery of "children of light," "clothed in Christ," "chosen," or "God's holy ones" are particularly appropriate. The gospel passages proclaimed may include the scrutiny gospels or those readings that express the baptismal call to love, to live according to God's ways, or to die and rise with Christ.

The communal celebration of the sacrament of Penance includes an examination of conscience after the homily. For this examination, areas of sinfulness voiced by the community during the Scrutiny preparation may be included effectively.

Involving the community in prayer through hymns and sung refrains throughout the time of individual confessions helps the assembly experience itself as community. The hymns chosen should reflect the community's renewal of its baptismal call to live as God's people and children of light.

Passion (Palm) Sunday

The profound celebration of Holy Week begins on Passion (Palm) Sunday. The elect and the baptized candidates may be given a special place in the procession as the community enters the church singing "Hosanna" and waving palm branches. The presider may remind the community of the presence of the elect and the candidates and encourage special prayer for them as they begin this final week of the journey to the Easter sacraments. The community, too, is reminded that this is a week of intense preparation to renew its own baptismal commitment.

Intercessions at all of the Masses on this day should reflect this time of immediate preparation both of the elect for the sacraments and of the entire community in the renewal of its own baptismal commitment.

The Easter Triduum

Members of the community who have shared the Lenten experience through small groups or with companions may choose to sit together at the liturgical celebrations during these three days. They may also spend time outside of the liturgy reflecting, praying, and sharing God's further work among them, which is celebrated in these liturgies.

As the community joins together in celebrating Christ's Passover through death to new life, the elect are brought into this powerful celebration of Christ's Paschal mystery. The elect share in the experience of the festive yet solemn atmosphere of the Mass of the Lord's Supper. Through the community's ritual action of foot washing, the elect experience this great act of Christian service. When dismissing the elect, the presider again makes it known that the elect and the community are journeying together toward their celebration of baptismal life in Christ. The community prays ardently for the elect.

At the Good Friday liturgy of the Lord's Passion, the elect are once again engulfed in a community passing through death with and in Christ. In the proclamation of the Word of God, the community and elect encounter the Body of Christ, blessed, broken, and poured out. In the reverencing of the cross, the community and elect together bring their own crosses carried to this moment of embracing the cross of Jesus. The Church's prayer and ritual provide a deep place for the elect to experience the living Body of Christ given for the life of the world. Once again in dismissing the elect the community sends them forth with conscious prayer until they assemble again to bathe in the waters of Christ's death and resurrection.

Holy Saturday has an ambience of quiet, of emptiness, of the stillness of death. Rather than being a day to complete Easter baskets, buy flowers, or clean the house for guests, it is a time for the community and elect to pray together to be more deeply open to the Risen Christ in the renewal and celebration of baptism. The entire church community is invited to attentive waiting at this time. The Paschal fast on Holy Saturday is to sustain an emptiness waiting to be filled with nothing less than Christ at the great eucharistic feast.

The parish community's prayer on Holy Saturday begins with morning prayer. Other forms of prayer and opportunities for sharing are also provided during the day. The focus of the prayer and sharing on this day is the significant moment of turning all over to Christ as the time of baptism and renewal of baptism nears. (See pages 136–137 in this manual for one such prayer possibility.) Other preparation rites for baptism may be celebrated in the midst of the community as well. (See pages 32–35 in this manual for further understanding of these preparation rites.)

PART TWO

Chapter 4
Reflection Sessions

Introduction

This chapter contains background material for the catechist on the Scriptures for the Sundays of Lent as well as Holy Thursday and Good Friday of the Easter Triduum. The session plans which follow each background essay then unfold in detail a process of spiritual reflection and sharing, based on the liturgy, which are designed to help participants come to a deeper conversion during this time of purification and enlightenment. The process of reflection begins with dismissal from the liturgy, which starts a half-hour period of reflection and then continues with an extended session, which can take place on the same day or on another day of the week.

The background material offers insights into the Word and explores images found in these Scripture passages which are relevant to the period of Purification and Enlightenment. The session plans which follow reflect the direction given in the Rite that this period is a "time for spiritual recollection" "consisting more in interior reflection than in catechetical instruction" (RCIA 7, 138–139). For this reason they are called *dismissal reflection* and *extended reflection* rather than *dismissal catechesis* and *extended catechesis*. These guided times of reflection take the place of catechetical sessions during this period.

Master copies of handouts which may be used in connection with these sessions are found in the appendix. They may be photocopied for the participants.

When the parish's catechumenal process includes unbaptized catechumens (called in this period *the elect*), Year A readings are proclaimed when the three rites of Scrutiny are celebrated, on the Third, Fourth, and Fifth Sunday of Lent. This is true even when the rest of the liturgical year employs readings from Year B or C. The lectionary readings for Year A are always to be used on these Sundays when there are elect preparing for baptism (RCIA,

146). The background material and sessions for Year A, therefore, would also be used on these Sundays for the gathering with the elect and any baptized candidates who may be preparing with them to celebrate the sacraments at Easter.

If the parish process in a given year has *only* baptized candidates, however, Year B and C readings would be used on the Third, Fourth, and Fifth Sunday of Lent according to the pattern of the rest of the liturgical year. Therefore, reflection sessions for these years of the lectionary cycle have also been provided. They are geared especially to the needs of the baptized candidates and do not include reflections on the Scrutinies.

When the parish's process includes baptized candidates, the Penitential Rite (RCIA, 459–472) is celebrated with them on the Second Sunday of Lent. All the sessions for the Second Sunday of Lent include a time when the participants may reflect on their experience of this rite. If there are no baptized candidates, or the rite is not celebrated at that time, the reflection pertaining to it can simply be omitted.

For each of these sessions, the catechist or another designated person prepares the space to be used ahead of time. The chairs are always arranged in a circle or semicircle. The focal point of the room is a table draped with a purple cloth upon which a candle is set. Some weeks the session contains a suggestion for an additional symbol to be used.

It is very important that these sessions be much more reflective in nature than are the catechetical sessions which give shape to the period of the catechumenate. They must include more time for quiet prayer and interior recollection. They are linked intimately with the powerful liturgical rites which occur throughout Lent. Indeed, these rites provide much of the stimulus for growth and reflection that the sessions then edify and further explore. This period is not a time to include everything else about Catholic teachings and practices. It is a time to be moved inwardly to deeper conversion.

First Sunday of Lent
Year A, B, and C

The Temptation of Jesus in the Desert

On this Sunday which opens the season of Lent, whether Year A, B, or C of the Lectionary is being proclaimed in the liturgy, the gospel account always places before the community the temptation of Jesus by Satan in the wilderness.

Year A Matthew 4:1–11	Year B Mark 1:12–15	Year C Luke 4:1–13

Year A
Matthew 4:1–11

In this account Satan is called the "tester" (*peirazon* in Greek), a title that evokes the testing of the Israelites in the wilderness, a test which the people failed. Jesus, however, does not succumb to the blandishments offered by Satan. He succeeds, and in this success the new Israel is launched.

In the original wandering through the wilderness, the people are challenged by Moses to keep faith (Deuteronomy 6–8) as they are tested—the language used for *covenant* refers to the Father-Son relationship. God is the parent and Israel is the beloved child. All these motifs are found in Matthew's account of the temptation: Son of God, testing, being led in the wilderness.

The Son of God, in whom we are all made children of heaven, creates the new Israel.

Year B
Mark 1:12–15

Sparse language characterizes Mark's entire Gospel. Details, therefore, stand out. In the temptation account Mark mentions "wild beasts" and "angels." These are used, perhaps, as apocalyptic figures, conveying the sense that Jesus' mission will be highly confrontational ("wild beasts"), a struggle between Jesus, who fights on behalf of heaven with divine power ("angels"), and the ways of a sinful world ("repent").

As this scene opens, Jesus is sent or thrust into the wilderness with a breathless, hurried urgency, which is characteristic of Mark's entire gospel account. This is, after all, war between good and evil.

Heaven wins the war ("This the time of fulfillment."), and here the battle lines are drawn.

Year C
Luke 4:1–13

The term used for Satan in this account is *devil* (*diabolis* in Greek), a title that conveys a sense of the chaotic, the diabolic, the agent who rips things apart as opposed to that which holds things together.

Satan is portrayed as having some power (*exousia* in Greek) in the diabolic kingdom, but Jesus, in refusing to be swayed and accept that which Satan offers, reveals the type of faithful, obedient Son he will be in fulfilling his mission, not claiming for himself pleasure, possessions, and glory. Rather, he will empty himself and triumph over evil on the cross at the final confrontation ("he left him, to await another opportunity").

In emptying himself for the sake of his mission, Jesus is "full of the Holy Spirit." After the temptation, in the fullness of this power, he proclaims good news to the people (Luke 4:14–21).

IMAGES OF PURIFICATION AND ENLIGHTENMENT

Election

It is God who does the choosing, God who forms and creates us (Year A first reading), establishes a relationship, a covenant with us (Year B first reading), and blesses us and brings us into a land flowing with milk and honey (Year C first reading). The people of God, the elect, achieve this status by the grace, mercy, and loving kindness of divine favor as offered in Jesus Christ.

Wilderness

The desert or wilderness is the location for the temptation of Jesus in all three gospel accounts. In such a barren landscape there are no distractions from the scrutiny of God's grace, love, and truth. Sometimes the place where temptation pulls at us most strongly is in the depths of the human heart.

And yet, the Spirit is always available to us to help us overcome temptation (in Mark's account Jesus is "driven" into the desert by the Spirit). Divine assistance is available to those who sift the experience of life by attempting to discern their direction and seeking to avoid doing evil instead of pursuing good.

Turning away from Satan/ Embracing God's Kingdom

In Matthew and Luke a dialogue takes place between the tempter and Jesus. Quotations from Scripture are hurled back and forth. Such a dialogue which uses Scripture to resolve issues is highly reminiscent of rabbinic debates. In that format, familiar to the first hearers of the Gospel, a powerful message is contained. Jesus renounces the entanglements of the devil and professes faith in God and the divine kingdom.

In the Rite of Baptism, the believer renounces Satan and sin and professes belief in the triune God. This renunciation and vowing takes place in the form of a dialogue. The questions are proposed and the believer responds, "I do!" In the account of Jesus' temptation in the desert a model is given for all believers who turn away from sin and embrace faith in God and the promises of the kingdom.

Right Relationship

The epistle readings for Years A and B focus on the disruption sin causes in our relationship with God and with one another, as does the first reading for Year A. The epistle reading for Year C focuses on a similar theme of alienation and the saving power of Jesus for all ("Jew and Greek") who confess belief. That which has been broken by sin has been healed in Christ. All those who have been divided and separated are brought together and made one in faith.

Fasting/Forty Days

Two gospel texts (Years A and C) for this Sunday open with Jesus fasting. As depicted in the Old Testament, both Moses and Elijah undertook a fast for forty days. Forty is mentioned in all three gospel accounts as the number of days that Jesus spent in the desert. A deliberate emptiness created by fasting from food is meant to physically remind the believer of one's dependence on God alone who fills us with good things and satisfies us. Forty is also a biblical symbol for a sufficiently long period of time. That which is undertaken in forty days is enough.

In God alone is our salvation. The allure of sin is powerful but cannot overwhelm the believer who holds fast to Jesus. For it is in the Lord Jesus that we conquer temptation. Satan's kingdom has been vanquished, and although we have from time to time wandered far from God, heaven has taken the initiative and in the Savior we are brought back and claimed for the kingdom of truth.

In this season we believers celebrate the strength which has been given us in Christ to purify our hearts and control our desires so that we might serve God in freedom.

(Ordinarily this session will take thirty minutes.)

Getting Started

1. Gather in the space that has been prepared ahead of time. Include a candle on a table.

2. Invite the elect and candidates to be seated. In silence, light the candle. Begin the prayer by speaking the name of each person and allowing for a moment of silence after each.

3. Continue the prayer with these or similar words:

   God, you created all things good.
   Today, we give thanks and praise for these elect and candidates whom you have called by name.
   Be with them in a special way as they begin this season of purification and enlightenment.
   Grant them the courage to face these forty days and the faith to know that you walk with them every step of the way.
   We ask this in the name of Jesus our brother who lives and reigns with you and the Holy Spirit, one God, forever and ever. Amen.

Initial Reflection

1. In a reflective manner, ask the elect and candidates to recall the Liturgy of the Word and the Rite of Sending, which have just been celebrated. After several minutes of silence, invite them to speak a word or phrase that describes the experience. Allow for quiet moments after each person speaks.

2. Continue the reflection using these or similar questions:

   - *What were you feeling and thinking as you heard your name spoken aloud?* (Pause for responses.)

   - *What were you feeling and thinking as you heard people give testimony on your behalf?* (Pause for responses.)

   - *What were you feeling and thinking when you wrote your name in the* Book of the Elect? (Pause for responses.)

3. Present a brief explanation of the term *election*, using these words or your own:

   God has called each of us by name. God has chosen each one of us and wants an intimate relationship with each person. Everyone is free to respond to God's invitation. Baptism establishes this relationship with each person because in baptism we become the adopted children of God. The Rite of Election *celebrates the Church's realization that God has called each of us by name and that each person freely chooses to enter into such a relationship with God. Thus signing the* Book of the Elect *is the immediate public act leading to baptism.*

4. Invite the candidates to name what they were feeling and thinking as they heard affirmation given on their behalf. Ask them what it means to them to realize that their names are already in the Book of the Elect. Help them to understand how significant it is that they have already been baptized and are already the adopted children of God and part of the community.

Prayer

Observe a period of silent prayer and conclude this segment by singing the song or acclamation that accompanied the signing of the Book of the Elect during the liturgy.

(Ordinarily this session will take sixty to ninety minutes.)

Processing

1. Have a member of the team bring the Book of the Elect to the group at the conclusion of the liturgy. Place the book on the table near the lighted candle.

2. Welcome the godparents, sponsors, and team members as they arrive. Ask everyone to be seated. In silence pass the book from person to person until everyone has had a few moments to look at the names in the book.

3. Invite everyone to share a word, phrase, or feeling about seeing the names in the book. Ask them to name other significant occasions which involve signing one's name, such as signing checks, taking out bank loans, closing on a house, getting a driver's or marriage license. Ask about the meaning of such a signature. Next, reflect with them why forgeries are so devastating to the person whose name has been forged.

4. Advance the discussion by asking what it meant to them to come forward and sign the book or for the candidates to know that their names are already in a Book of the Elect. Be attuned to such words as *covenant, commitment, responsibility.*

5. Reflect with the group on the importance of one's name and that it is the means by which we are individually known by other people and by God. Also reflect with them on this statement: Our name is the only thing we take with us when we die and it is by our name that we are remembered by family and friends.

6. Ask the elect and candidates to pair off with their godparents and sponsors to reflect and share their thoughts on the following:

    • The significance of their name, who they might be named after, others with the same name that they admire, saints who bear the same name or a derivative thereof;

    • What it means to be called by name, by God, by this community;

    • In what ways they respond to this call to be disciples engaged in mission.

7. After fifteen to twenty minutes, invite them to reassemble. Ask if anyone would like to summarize in a word or phrase what has been shared.

Putting Faith into Practice

1. Spend a few minutes discussing or briefly reviewing (if they have already had an opportunity to learn about Lent) the meaning of the season of Lent and its practices of prayer, fasting, and works of charity.

2. Present an explanation of Lent as a retreat time, which means a slowing down, a stepping aside to reflect on one's life to sift through one's attitudes, decisions, and actions in order to determine what is of God, for which we give thanks, and what is sinful, for which we ask forgiveness and the strength to change.

3. Restate the benefits of keeping a journal, of seeking spiritual guidance, of fasting, of doing works of charity, and of sharing and praying frequently with godparents or sponsors.

4. Encourage them to participate in the parish community's Lenten opportunities.

5. Invite them to spend some time in quiet now to begin their retreat experience for forty days and, if there is time, to begin to share with their godparents or sponsors.

Prayer

Invite everyone to observe a moment of quiet and to speak to God in their heart, giving thanks to God for calling them by name and asking for God's help in a special way during the season of Lent. Conclude with a prayer of your own or use the responsorial psalm or a song from the Liturgy.

(Ordinarily this session will take thirty minutes.)

Getting Started

1. Gather in the space that has been prepared ahead of time, which includes one or two desert items such as a pottery bowl with sand, a small cactus, or a dead branch.

2. Ask the elect and candidates to be seated. After some silence, pray in these or similar words:

   God of day and God of darkness, be with us in a special way during this holy season of Lent.
   Open our minds and hearts to hear your message of truth, hope, and love.
   Help us to see with the eyes of faith and recognize the many gifts you have given to us especially the gift of your Son, Jesus.
   Give us the grace we need to withstand the power of Satan, in particular the temptation to doubt your love and faithfulness.
   We ask this through Christ our Lord. Amen.

Initial Reflection

1. Invite the elect and candidates to speak a word or phrase which describes their experience of today's liturgy. Encourage them to include what they observed, heard, or sensed in the liturgy and its surroundings. Be attuned to such words as *desert, wilderness, temptation, Satan, forty days of fasting,* and *prayer.* Connect their words to the annual observance of Lent and its place in the liturgical year.

2. Reflect with the participants on the experience of being called by name saying:

   What were you feeling and thinking as you heard your name spoken aloud? (Pause for responses.)
   What were you feeling and thinking as you heard people give testimony on your behalf? (Pause for responses.)
   What were you feeling and thinking as you entered your name in the Book of the Elect? (Pause for responses.)

3. Consult Chapter 2 concerning the Rite of Election. Present a brief explanation of the term *election* using these words or your own:

   God has called each of us by name. God has chosen every one of us and wants an intimate relationship with each person. Everyone is free to respond to God's invitation. Baptism establishes this relationship with each person because in baptism we become the adopted children of God. The Rite of Election *celebrates the Church's realization that God has called each of us by name and each person freely chooses to enter into such a relationship with God. Thus signing the* Book of the Elect *is the immediate public act leading to baptism.*

4. Invite the candidates to name what they were feeling and thinking as they heard affirmation given on their behalf. Ask them what it means to them to realize that their names are already in the Book of the Elect. Help them to appreciate the significance of their baptism.

Prayer

Return to an atmosphere of quiet. After several minutes, sing or play the song "Be Not Afraid" (Robert Dufford, SJ, New Dawn Music, 1975).

(Ordinarily this session will take sixty to ninety minutes.)

Processing

1. Welcome godparents, sponsors, spouses, and other team members. Invite the elect and candidates to be seated with their godparents and sponsors beside them. In silence, take the bowl of sand to each one, asking them to touch the sand or to move it around in the bowl. Invite all to close their eyes, take a few deep breaths, and imagine being in a desert or wilderness.

2. Proclaim the Gospel.

3. After several minutes of quiet, continue with a guided meditation such as:

   In the distance, from two directions, two figures begin to emerge. You observe that both are well dressed, striking in appearance, and focused on you. As they approach, they greet you by name and welcome you to their neighborhood. One is very solicitous of your needs, promises that all of what you think you need plus more than you can imagine will be yours if you are willing to spend your life working for his organization. The other waits patiently, but his presence permeates the area. You feel his presence. There is something so kind and so gentle about him. He does not promise an easy journey or quick rewards. He does promise to walk with you every step of the journey. The decision is yours. You ponder what to do. How do you choose?

4. Proclaim the Gospel again. After some silence, ask the elect and candidates to go with their godparents and sponsors to a corner of the room or for a walk for fifteen to twenty minutes to discuss:

   - What the desert/wilderness are. What the temptations are that are so present to each of us and to our world.

   - How to recognize what is of God and what is evil.

   - The need to renounce sin and to profess faith in God each and every day.

5. Gather everyone back and have them form into a circle. Invite anyone who wishes to summarize in a sentence or two what has been shared. Affirm the various aspects of Lent that might emerge. For example:

   - Lent is a time to reflect on the direction our life is going and to determine what is of God and what is sinful.

   - Lent is a time for individuals, parish communities, and the whole Church to reflect on how the gospel message of Jesus Christ is being preached and practiced in daily living.

   - Lent is a season to change behaviors that lead us away from God and to deepen behaviors that lead us toward God.

   - Lent is a time to reflect on God's grace and faithfulness.

Putting Faith into Practice

1. Share with the group the various Lenten opportunities that are available within the parish and outside of it.

2. Remind the elect and candidates to be faithful to writing in their journals.

3. Encourage them to meet frequently with their godparents or sponsors for prayer and discussion of their experience of Lent.

4. Review the traditional Lenten practices of prayer, fasting and works of charity, and the ways in which the local community supports these practices.

Prayer

Invite everyone to form into a circle with the godparents and sponsors behind their respective elect or candidate. After a few moments of silence, invite anyone who wishes to pray aloud in their own words. (Be ready with a prayer of your own.) Conclude by singing the responsorial psalm, an acclamation, or a song from today's liturgy.

(Ordinarily this session will take thirty minutes.)

Getting Started

1. Gather in the space that has been prepared ahead of time and invite everyone to be seated.

2. After a few moments of silence, sing or play "God Has Chosen Me" (Bernadette Farrell, OCP Publications, Inc., 1990).

Initial Reflection

1. Ask the elect and candidates to reflect on the Liturgy of the Word and the Rite of Sending, which have just been celebrated. After several minutes of silence, invite volunteers to speak a word or phrase that describes their experience. Allow for quiet moments after each person speaks.

2. Discuss the experience of being called by name. Ask what they were feeling and thinking as they heard their names spoken aloud. Explore further what the experience was for them as they heard people give testimony on their behalf. Ask what they were feeling and thinking when they entered their name in the Book of the Elect.

3. Present a brief explanation of the term *election* using these words or your own:

   > *God has called each of us by name. God has chosen each one of us and wants an intimate relationship with each person. Everyone is free to respond to God's invitation. Baptism establishes this relationship with each person because in baptism we become the adopted children of God. The* Rite of Election *celebrates the Church's realization that God has called each of us by name and that each person freely chooses to enter into such a relationship with God. Thus signing the* Book of the Elect *is the immediate public act leading to baptism.*

4. Invite the candidates to name what they were feeling and thinking as they heard affirmation being given on their behalf. Ask them what it means to them to realize that their names are already in the Book of the Elect. Help them to appreciate the significance of their baptism and that they are already the adopted children of God.

Prayer

Invite everyone to be quiet and to spend a few minutes speaking to God in the quiet of their hearts. Sing or play again "God Has Chosen Me."

(Ordinarily this session will take sixty to ninety minutes.)

Processing

1. Welcome godparents, sponsors, and others to the group. Invite them to share with one another what each is feeling or thinking as the Church begins once again the celebration of the season of Lent.

2. After a few minutes, invite everyone to enter into a moment of quiet time. Proclaim the Gospel followed by a few more minutes of quiet.

3. Review with them that Lent is a time to step back, to retreat, in order to look at our lives and to determine how we are doing at living out or preparing to live out our baptismal promises. Deliberately, with pauses after each question, voice the baptismal promises. Say in these or similar words:

   These promises cause us to reflect on our relationship with God and to reflect on the reality of temptation and sin in our lives, in our society, and in our communities. We reflect on whether we are in right relationship with God, people, and things; and if we are not in a right relationship, we are invited to use the season of Lent to do something about getting back into a right relationship through prayer, fasting, and works of charity.

4. Proclaim the Gospel again.

5. Invite the elect and candidates to pair off with their respective godparents and sponsors to discuss:

   - My relationship with God is . . .
     What can I do to strengthen my relationship with God?

   - My relationships with other people are . . .
     What can I do to better my relationships with other people? What works of charity would help to put me in right relationships with other people?

   - My relationships with things are . . .
     What can I do to have a better balance in my relationship with things? What type of fasting would help me to bring about harmony in my relationships with things?

6. After twenty minutes or so, gather everyone back together. Invite volunteers to speak about their sharing. Summarize Lent as a time of retreat to look at our relationship with God, others, and things.

Putting Faith into Practice

1. Encourage everyone to journal frequently about their relationship with God, others, and things.

2. Review the parish opportunities available during Lent.

3. Encourage frequent meetings between elect and godparent and candidate and sponsor for prayer and sharing about the Lenten journey.

Prayer

Invite everyone to enter into a moment of quiet time. Ask them to speak to God in the quiet of their hearts about their desires, fears, and expectations of this Lent. You and other team members go to each elect and candidate, lay your hands on their heads and quietly pray that God will help them in a special way this Lent. Invite godparents and sponsors to do the same. If possible, play instrumental music softly as the laying on of hands is done.

Second Sunday of Lent
Year A, B, and C

The Transfiguration of Jesus on the Mountain

On this Sunday which follows the temptation of Jesus in the desert—whether Year A, B, or C of the Lectionary is being proclaimed in the liturgy—the gospel account always places before the community the Transfiguration of Jesus on the mountain. It would be helpful to contrast various details in the three synoptic accounts.

Year A Matthew 17:1–9	Year B Mark 9:2–10	Year C Luke 9:28–36
Only in Matthew do we read that Jesus' face "became as dazzling as the sun." This may relate to an earlier reference in the Gospel to the righteous who will shine like the sun in the kingdom of God (Matthew 13:43) and to the brilliantly shining face of Moses after the revelation on Sinai (Exodus 34:29).	By the use of a characteristic literary device ("Jesus . . . led them up a high mountain."), Mark signals that a special teaching or revelation is about to happen.	Luke is the only evangelist to describe the events of the Transfiguration of Jesus as occurring after prayer, just as he reports the revelation occurring at the baptism of Jesus—after prayer.
In this account Peter avoids the title *Rabbi* in referring to Jesus and instead calls him *Lord* (*kyrios* in Greek). Rabbi was an important term that was used among the disciples' opponents (Matthew 23:8), and it is how Judas addresses Jesus when he betrays him (Matthew 26:25).	Only Mark includes the detail about Jesus' clothes becoming dazzling white, "such as no one on earth could bleach them." This may be alluding to the clothing of the angel who speaks with Daniel, encouraging him about the future of God's people (Daniel 10:5–21). Martyrs were also described as wearing white robes. The "young man" who flees naked at the arrest of Jesus (Mark 14:52) is unwilling to go to the cross with him; however, later a young man sits clothed in white in the tomb at the place of honor because he has "died" with Jesus in baptism.	Unique to Luke's account is the reference to Jesus' passage or "departure" (*exodus* in Greek), which he was about to accomplish at Jerusalem. This is meant to recall the Exodus event and link Jesus' suffering, death, resurrection, and ascension to the exodus experience of God's people. In Jesus, the "chosen" of God (unlike the other accounts in which the term "beloved" is used) we experience an "exodus" and the "passing over" into the new life of the kingdom. By his Resurrection-Ascension the Spirit is released upon the Church, the chosen of God.
Later, after the event of the cross, the disciples will be sustained (and understand) what occurs in this vision (*horama* in Greek) of the Transfiguration.		

IMAGES OF PURIFICATION AND ENLIGHTENMENT

Mountain

Mountains offer a vantage point, a location above the lower terrain that stretch one's view of the horizon beyond what is normally available on the flatlands. People can see more from the top of the mountain. Perhaps this is why mountains figure so prominently in both the Old and New Testaments.

On the mountaintop the divine presence is not only encountered but a special revelation is given. For example, the revelation to Moses for all God's people is given at Mount Sinai and the "whispering voice" occurs at the mouth of the cave for Elijah. In Year B, the first reading concerning the sacrifice of Isaac is also set on a mountain ("a height"). Because of his faith and obedience to the command of God, Abraham is blessed with the promise of a covenant.

Conversation with Moses and Elijah

Jesus appears to be speaking with Moses and Elijah, two heroes of God's people who symbolize all of the covenant relationship and tradition of the people of Israel: the Law and the Prophets. Also, in the figure of Elijah there are some apocalyptic overtones, since in Jesus' day there was a belief that the Messiah's coming would be prefigured by Elijah's return.

Glory

In each evangelist's account of the Transfiguration there are details which underscore the glory which is beheld by the three privileged disciples: Peter, John, and James. The appearance of Jesus changes: his face dazzles them (Matthew), his clothes become impossibly white (Mark), and while both of those details are repeated in Luke, the term *glory* is used to describe Moses' and Elijah's appearance. The disciples are filled with awe and fear at this manifestation.

Each synoptic account of the Transfiguration is preceded by Jesus teaching on the condition of discipleship, which entails denying oneself and taking up the cross. Given this context, clearly, the Transfiguration prefigures the true glory of the Messiah who has come to suffer and die for the sake of the kingdom. This is the glory to which we are all called as disciples of Christ. Thus, in the second reading from Year A, Paul instructs Timothy and the community to "bear your share of the hardship which the Gospel entails."

The changed appearance of Jesus on the mountaintop is also a glimpse of the future glory that all believers will share in the fullness of the kingdom. Thus, in the second reading for Year B, Paul writes to the Church at Rome, saying that the crucified One who has been raised up now sits at the "right hand of God," which is the place of glory. In Year C, the second reading from Paul's letter to the Philippians holds out to us believers the promise of a "glorified body."

Dazzling or White Robe

The appearance of Jesus' robe may contain hints of both glorification and martyrdom. The last book of the Christian Scriptures (Revelation) speaks of the multitude of the elect standing around the throne of God dressed in white robes and holding palm branches—a sign of victory. In early Christian iconography, the martyrs are depicted as wearing white robes.

Those who have been newly baptized and thus incorporated into the mystery of Jesus' saving death and resurrection are robed in white. The purified life that they have now entered into is meant to be kept free from the stain of sin until the return to this world of the Lord Jesus for a second time in glory.

The disciples were given a glimpse of the glory of Jesus prior to his suffering and death on the cross. The way of Jesus is the way of the cross, and the glory of the Resurrection and new life comes at the cost of suffering. The fulfillment of the Law and the Prophets is found in Jesus, who is our passover into the glories of the kingdom of God. This is the message and the teaching imparted on the holy mountain of God's transfiguring love and truth.

In this season, believers celebrate the hope to which we are called, the journey of changed appearances that signals inner growth and the rich renewal of our hearts and minds. Our

(Ordinarily this session will take thirty minutes.)

Getting Started

1. Gather in the space that has been prepared ahead of time. Include a white cloth laid over the purple cloth and a candle.
2. Invite the elect and candidates to be seated in silence. Light the candle. After several moments of silence pray in these or similar words:

   Savior God, Creator of life, we give thanks and praise to you for the blessings of this holy season of Lent.

   Grant in us the desire to be transformed to new life in and through the power of the cross.

   Help us to maintain hope in the promise of Jesus Christ our Lord, who lives and reigns with you and the Holy Spirit, one God, forever and ever. Amen.

Initial Reflection

1. Elicit from the elect and candidates a word, phrase, or feeling from today's liturgy or the mood of the celebration.
2. Reflect with the participants images, places, and people from the liturgy such as a mountain, white or dazzling robe, conversation with Elijah and Moses. Have them discuss what these images and persons convey about who Jesus is and his glory.
3. Ask about the message they heard proclaimed in the liturgy and what it imparted about the challenge of discipleship and the meaning of this holy season of Lent.

Alternative: If the Penitential Rite has been celebrated, use this process for the initial reflection:

1. Ask the elect and candidates to reflect on the Liturgy of the Word and the Penitential Rite just celebrated. After several minutes of silence, invite them to speak a word or phrase that describes the experience. Allow for quiet moments after each person speaks.
2. Lead the participants in a reflective recollection of the liturgy. For example:

   Close your eyes and remember arriving at church this morning. What were you thinking or feeling? (Pause. Hum a few lines of the gathering song.)

   Father greeted us; we were seated for the proclamation of the Word. (Say a few words or phrases from the readings and responsorial psalm. Include a few words and phrases from the homily. Pause.)

   Then Father invited us to pray. Recall your feelings as you knelt down, and as you heard the intercessions prayed (sung). (Pause.)

   A prayer was prayed for the candidates. Hands were laid on their heads. A prayer to Jesus was invoked with hands outstretched. (Pause.)

   (Perhaps a song was sung.) And then you were sent forth with a blessing. (Pause.)

3. Invite the candidates to share what they felt, thought, or experienced during the Penitential Rite. Then invite the elect to share what they experienced as they witnessed this rite.
4. Invite them to reflect on conversion. In these or similar words define it:

   Conversion is a turning to the person of Jesus Christ. The journey of conversion results in our realization of the reality of sin and the need to die to sin in order to rise with Jesus Christ. Conversion involves the recognition of the glory of the Resurrection. Conversion is a lifelong journey supported and nourished in and through the community.

5. Invite them to pair off and share their conversion experience. After some time, gather them back together. Elicit comments from their shared experiences. Listen carefully in order to reflect back to the group some of their key words and phrases that relate to God's grace, the gift of Jesus Christ, and the support of the community. Allow for quiet moments after each person speaks.

Prayer

Invite everyone to enter into a moment of quiet time and to speak to Jesus in the quiet of their hearts.

(Ordinarily this session will take sixty to ninety minutes.)

Processing

1. Welcome godparents, sponsors, and other team members. After asking everyone to enter into a few moments of quiet time, proclaim the Gospel from today's liturgy.
2. Discuss the mountain as a place for encountering God as Abraham, Moses, and Elijah did. Ask them to name other encounters described in the Bible that take place on a mountain.
3. Describe the covenant relationship between God and the Israelites, particularly as it is described by the whole Exodus experience, the journey of freedom from Egypt into the Promised Land. Speak about Jesus as the giver of the new covenant relationship established between God and us. Discuss the insight that for any relationship to continue it is important for the people in the relationship to spend time with one another.
4. Lead a simple meditation. Ask everyone to get comfortable, to close their eyes, and to take several deep breaths. Lead them slowly and deliberately in the following meditation:

   Imagine yourself in a beautiful setting in nature. Notice the grass, trees, water, the warmth or coolness of the air around you. Feel the day. You see a path in the distance and are attracted to it. The path winds up a hill or mountain. You begin to walk up the path. The view is spectacular. Just ahead you see a rock to sit on. Seated, you just look around at all the beauty. Quietly, but not suddenly, someone approaches and greets you by name. You look up to see Jesus. You invite him to sit with you. The two of you have a wonderful heart-to-heart conversation. Allow five minutes or more, then continue. *After awhile, Jesus gets up to leave. As he does so, he blesses you. In a few minutes, you too get up and return down the hill or mountain. You come back to this place and time.*

   Invite everyone to open their eyes.
5. Ask the elect and the candidates to pair off with their godparents or sponsors to discuss what the meditation experience was like for them: What was it like to have time alone with Jesus and to hear the words or message Jesus communicated to you? After fifteen minutes or so, invite everyone to gather together and ask volunteers to share their responses with the entire group.
6. Discuss the importance of taking time to pray and to reflect on their relationship with Christ.

Putting Faith into Practice

1. Provide everyone with the opportunity to reflect on the Lenten journey they have made thus far by asking them to ponder one of the following:
   - Name someone or something from this past week which helped you recall God's invitation to you to walk this Lenten journey. Reflect on how such an encounter affirmed and/or challenged you.
   - Recall last week's celebration of the Rite of Election and God's calling you by name. In what ways did you continue to hear God choosing you this week and how did you respond to that choice?
   - Name the ways you have tried to carry out the Lenten practices of prayer, fasting, and works of charity this past week. How did such practices help you become more aware of God's presence with you as well as the reality of your struggle with sin and temptation?

   After ten minutes of quiet, invite volunteers to name insights gained from their reflection.

Prayer

Ask everyone to enter into a few moments of quiet time by taking a few deep breaths. Invite anyone who wishes to pray aloud. After the last person has prayed, conclude by singing or reading aloud hymn 1 (1 Peter 1:3–5) found in "Hymns in the Style of the New Testament," *RCIA, Appendix II: Acclamations, Hymns and Songs,* RCIA, 596.1.

(Ordinarily this session will take thirty minutes.)

Getting Started

1. Gather in the space that has been prepared ahead of time. Include for this Sunday a cross and a white cloth laid over the purple cloth.

2. Invite the elect and candidates to be seated. In silence light the candle, pick up the cross and present it to each person, allowing each person a few moments to take it, hold it, and look at it.

3. Return the cross to the table and be seated for a few more moments in silence.

Initial Reflection

1. Invite the elect and candidates to reflect on the Liturgy of the Word that has just been celebrated. After a few minutes, invite each person to say a word, or phrase, or describe a feeling they recall from the Liturgy. Deepen the reflection by asking them to name what that word, phrase, or feeling conveys about conversion.

2. Explore conversion with them by asking *what* conversion involves, *who* it involves, and *how long* it takes. Stress that conversion is at the heart of their journey of faith and that it involves the whole person: head, heart, hands, and feet.

3. Ponder with them the connection between conversion and transfiguration which we celebrate every year on the Second Sunday of Lent. Use these or similar words:

   Conversion is a turning toward God, a God who is always reaching out to us by name. Conversion challenges us to look at our relationship with God and to name what in that relationship needs to be transformed in us in order to deepen that relationship. Conversion leads to transfiguration in the manner in which Saint Paul describes: "It is no longer I who lives but Christ who lives in me."

   Remind them that Lent is a season when the whole Church seeks to be renewed in its conversion to Jesus Christ.

Prayer

Invite everyone to sit quietly and to speak to Jesus in the silence of their hearts.

Alternative: If the Penitential Rite has been celebrated use this process:

1. Ask the elect and candidates to reflect on the Liturgy of the Word and the Penitential Rite that has just been celebrated. After several minutes of silence, invite everyone to speak a word or phrase that describes the experience. Allow for quiet moments after each person speaks.

2. Lead the participants in a reflective recollection of the liturgy. For example:

   Close your eyes and remember arriving at church this morning. What were you thinking or feeling? (Pause. Hum a few lines of the gathering song.)

   Father greeted us; we were seated for the proclamation of the Word. (Say a few words or phrases from the readings and responsorial psalm. Include a few words and phrases from the homily. Pause.)

   Then Father invited us to pray. Remember what it was like to kneel down and to hear the intercessions, which we helped to write, prayed (chanted or sung). (Pause.) A prayer was prayed, hands were laid on the heads of the candidates, a prayer to Jesus was invoked with hands outstretched. (Pause.) And then you were sent forth with a blessing. (Pause.)

3. Invite the candidates to share what they felt, thought, or experienced during the Penitential Rite. Then invite the elect to share their experiences as well.

4. Invite them to reflect on conversion. In these or similar words define it:

   Conversion is a turning to the person of Jesus Christ. The journey of conversion results in our realization of the reality of sin and the need to die to sin in order to rise with Jesus Christ. Conversion involves the recognition of the glory of the Resurrection. Conversion is a lifelong journey supported and nourished in and through the community.

5. Invite everyone to pair off and share their experience of conversion. After some time, gather them back together. Elicit comments about what was shared in the reflection. Listen carefully in order to reflect back to the group some of their key words and phrases that relate to God's grace, the gift of Jesus Christ, and the support of the community. Allow for quiet moments after each person speaks.

Prayer

Invite everyone to become silent. Repeat the words of any one passage from the prayer over the candidates used in the Rite (RCIA, 470). Sing a song or acclamation from the Liturgy of the Word.

EXTENDED REFLECTION FOR YEAR B

(Ordinarily this session will take sixty to ninety minutes.)

Processing

1. Welcome the godparents, sponsors and other team members. Invite everyone to be seated.
2. After a few moments of silence proclaim the Gospel from today's liturgy.
3. Direct everyone to look at handout 5, which has these points for reflection:
    * Reflect on your experience of this initiation process. In light of your experience, name ways you have been transfigured or transformed.
    * Reflect and name what remains to be transformed.
    * Just as Peter, James, and John saw a new dimension of Jesus manifested, what new aspects of Jesus are being manifested to you? In what ways are these occurring?
    * In the gospel reading, the voice told the disciples that Jesus is God's Son, the Chosen One, and that they were to listen to him. Listen with your heart. What does Jesus say to you? What do you need or desire?
4. After fifteen to twenty minutes of silent reflection, invite the elect and candidates to pair off and share their reflection with their respective godparent and sponsor.
5. In ten minutes or so, gather everyone back together into a circle and ask for volunteers to share words or phrases from their reflection and sharing.
6. Discuss the Transfiguration of Jesus and its glory, using these words or your own:
    The Transfiguration provides us with a glimpse of the glory of Jesus Christ. The way of Jesus is the way of the cross and the glory of the Resurrection; new life comes at the cost of suffering. In this season we believers celebrate the hope to which we are called, the journey of conversion which signals inner growth and the rich renewal of our hearts and minds. Our destiny as disciples is the glory of Christ.

Putting Faith into Practice

1. Review with everyone that the season of Lent is a time to reflect on how we are living as disciples of Jesus. It is a time to name what is of God and to be affirmed; it is also a time to name what is sinful and in need of transformation.
2. Encourage everyone to continue to write in their journals this week, focusing on discipleship and its implications for the workplace and the home.
3. Review also the traditional Lenten practices of prayer, fasting, and works of charity.

Prayer

Ask each person to think about how they would complete this petition:

> *Lord Jesus, I ask that you transform in me . . . so that I may share in your glory.*

Give everyone some time to think about their petition. Invite volunteers to pray aloud their petition. Conclude by singing a song or acclamation from the Liturgy of the Word.

(Ordinarily this session will take thirty minutes.)

Getting Started

1. Gather in the space that has been prepared ahead of time. Include for this Sunday a cross and a white cloth laid over the purple cloth.
2. Invite the elect and candidates to be seated. Pray in these or similar words:

   Jesus, you chose to come down to earth to be as one of us.

   You became for us the way, the truth, and the life.

   You showed us how to live as God's chosen people, willing to lay down our life for others just as you laid down your life for us.

   Help us to keep our eyes fixed on our destiny, which is eternal life with you.

   Help us not to be led astray by temptations, in particular the temptation to doubt life everlasting with you.

   Help us to become transformed as your disciples here on earth so that one day we may all be united with you and all the saints and angels.

   We ask this in your name, now and forever. Amen.

Initial Reflection

1. Recall the Liturgy of the Word that has just been celebrated. Use the songs which were sung, words from the opening prayer, phrases or words from the readings of the day, and key thoughts and phrases from the homily.
2. Invite the elect and candidates to pair off and discuss what they heard proclaimed and what they experienced in today's liturgy.
3. After some time ask the pairs to write a sentence or two summarizing the message they want to remember from today's liturgy.
4. Call on each group to share their summary and comment as appropriate.

Prayer

Sing or listen to "Jerusalem, My Destiny" (Rory Cooney, GIA Publications Inc., 1990).

Alternative: If the Penitential Rite has been celebrated, use this process:

1. Ask the elect and candidates to reflect on the Liturgy of the Word and the Penitential Rite that has just been celebrated. After several minutes of silence, invite them to speak a word or phrase that describes the experience. Allow for quiet moments after each person speaks.
2. Lead the participants in a reflective recollection of the liturgy. For example:

   Close your eyes and remember arriving at church this morning. What were you thinking or feeling? (Pause. Hum a few lines of the gathering song.)

   Father greeted us; we were seated for the proclamation of the Word. (Say a few words or phrases from the readings and responsorial psalm. Include a few words and phrases from the homily. Pause.)

   Then Father invited us to pray. Recall how it felt to kneel down, to hear the intercessions, which we helped to write, prayed (sung or chanted). (Pause.)

   A prayer was prayed, hands were laid on the heads of the candidates, a prayer to Jesus was invoked, with hands outstretched. (Pause.)

   And then you were sent forth with a blessing. (Pause.)

3. Invite the candidates to share what they felt, thought, or experienced during the Penitential Rite. Then invite the elect to share as well.
4. Invite them to reflect on conversion. In these or similar words define it:

   Conversion is a turning to the person of Jesus Christ. The journey of conversion results in our realization of the reality of sin and the need to die to sin in order to rise with Jesus Christ. Conversion involves the recognition of the glory of the Resurrection. Conversion is a lifelong journey supported and nourished in and through the community.

5. Invite everyone to pair off and share their experience of conversion. After some time, gather them back together. Elicit comments about what was shared in the reflection. Listen carefully in order to reflect back to the group

some of their key words and phrases that relate to God's grace, the gift of Jesus Christ, and the support of the community. Allow for quiet moments after each person speaks.

Prayer

Sing or listen to "Jerusalem, My Destiny" (Rory Cooney, GIA Publications, Inc., 1990).

EXTENDED REFLECTION FOR YEAR C

(Ordinarily this session will take sixty to ninety minutes.)

Processing

1. Welcome the godparents, sponsors, and other team members. Ask the elect and candidates to be seated in pairs with their respective godparent or sponsor.
2. After a few moments of silence, proclaim the second reading from today's liturgy. After a significant pause, proclaim the Gospel, followed by another lengthy moment of silence.
3. Invite the pairs to discuss words, phrases, images, or feelings contained in the readings and to share ideas about what those words, phrases, images, or feelings convey about discipleship and its costs for the church community as well as each person.
4. After some time, ask for feedback from the pairs about their discussion.
5. Comment about the dazzling or white robe of the transfigured Jesus and its connection with "the elect" standing before the throne of God in white robes. Comment further regarding the white robe as the sign of baptism, our dying to sin and rising to new life (glory) in Jesus Christ.
6. Stress that during this season of Lent, the Church offers us opportunities to reflect on the great gift of God: Jesus, God's only Son, who became one of us and came down to live among us to give us hope, to show us the way, and to assure us that the Spirit would be with us until the end of time.
7. Invite the pairs to discuss the rewards of a life of discipleship which they already are experiencing, as well as the reward promised to all who remain faithful to the mission of Jesus Christ.
8. After some time, again ask for feedback from the pairs regarding their discussion.
9. Provide some guidance for continued reflection and discussion throughout the coming week by stressing the importance of embracing one's cross, whether it is a personal or a communal cross. Also encourage everyone to reflect on the glimpses of the glory of Christ and his assurance that we will not be abandoned.

Putting Faith into Practice

1. Encourage everyone to leaf through the newspaper this week, looking for the signs of the glory of God when the love of neighbor is practiced.
2. Invite them to reflect on the journey of faith which they have thus far taken and have them note aspects of transformation which have occurred in their lives, as well as aspects still in need of transformation. Invite those who are willing to share these aspects of their transformation with their godparents or sponsors.
3. Review the Lenten practices of prayer, fasting, works of charity, and almsgiving.

Prayer

Invite the elect and candidates to form an inner circle with the godparents, sponsors, and other team members standing behind them. Ask the godparents and sponsors to place their hands on the shoulders of their elect or candidate and in silence to pray for him or her.

After a few minutes, go to each elect and candidate and bless them upon their forehead with the sign of the cross, saying "May you come to share in the glory of Christ." Close the prayer with "Jerusalem, My Destiny" or another appropriate song.

Third Sunday of Lent
Year A

The Samaritan Woman at the Well

Exodus 17:3–7
Psalm 95:1–2, 6–9
Romans 5:1–2, 5–8
John 4:5–42

No matter what year is correct in the lectionary cycle, when the first Scrutiny is celebrated the readings are taken from Year A (Lectionary, 745). Taken together, the readings for the first Scrutiny are clearly characterized by a water or baptismal theme, especially when seen through the lens of the gospel text of Jesus' encounter with the Samaritan woman at the well.

The woman arrives at the site of Jacob's Well to draw water as Jesus is passing through Samaria. Jesus is bold in addressing her, for most rabbis in Jesus' day assiduously avoided interaction with women in public. In addition, she is a Samaritan, an impure people shunned because of their inter-marriage with pagans, idolatry, and rejection of the Temple worship located in Jerusalem. The dialogue which ensues is held on two levels and is charac-teristic of John's Gospel where an image (for example, light, bread, or birth) is used by Jesus to communicate on a higher or spiritual truth while the unenlightened understand this same image on a lower or natural level. In this instance the image is that of water. Jesus offers "living water" to the woman. She first does not understand and asks for this water so that she will not grow thirsty again. The water that Jesus will give is not that which is contained or hemmed in by a well but living water, the fountain welling up from within a person to provide authentic life in the Spirit.

In this long dialogue between the woman and Jesus, her use of titles for Jesus suggests a growing faith, a growth which is assisted by Jesus' responses. She calls him "a Jew," then "Sir" (the term *kyrois* in Greek can also imply *Lord*), then "a prophet," and finally "the Messiah." Many have interpreted the woman's use of these terms as signals of a gradually dawning faith in a sinner ostracized for her many marriages and current unmarried relationship. Another inter-pretation is that she is not held in contempt at all, otherwise the village would not listen to her as she excitedly tells them of meeting the one who could be the Messiah. The reference to husbands (*husband* in Hebrew is *ba'al*) could also function as a symbol in that the *baalim* were the five gods or idols of Samaria. This woman who encounters Jesus can thus be seen as searching or thirsting for God but looking in the wrong place. Jesus offers her "worship in spirit and truth" in his own person ("I am he, the one who is speaking with you," NAB), unmistakably echoing the self-revelation of God to Moses on Sinai (Exodus 3:14).

Searcher and leader that she is, the woman is not afraid to engage Jesus, to ask him questions, and to challenge him (unlike the disciples who are surprised to find him speaking to a woman and who would not question him). Her stance before Jesus underscores that those who seek the living waters do not "talk among themselves" (as did the Twelve after the encounter), but they actively and fearlessly engage the teacher and the master. In that dialogue with the Lord, the disciple will learn, grow, and come to true faith.

After speaking with Jesus, the woman leaves behind her water jar, perhaps a symbol of her former idolatry, and convinces the village to give this wandering rabbi a hearing. Her witness to Jesus enables others to also come to faith. Behind the refer-ence to "fields shining for harvest" may lie baptismal imagery (the shining white robes of newly initiated). This further explains the role of the true disciple as an evangelizer, one who hands on the Good News of Jesus to others that faith may grow and be harvested.

IMAGES OF PURIFICATION AND ENLIGHTENMENT

Thirst

In the first reading, the people complain to Moses of their thirst. They rail against God, whom they believe has abandoned them to die in the desert. Thirst, in the harsh and threatening dryness of the desert environment, is a metaphor for the human dependence upon God. When God responds to the people's complaint, Moses is instructed to strike the rock upon which the Lord would stand and water would flow. Some rabbis, in commenting on the Scripture, likened the rock to the Torah and its tradition. What slakes the thirst and fills with faith is the Law and tradition, which will guide people through this world and the desert into the Promised Land.

Reading the gospel text in conjunction with the first reading, commentators will apply the image of thirst to the Samaritan woman. Her thirst for authentic faith was filled by Jesus. While this may be an appropriate application in harmonizing the readings, this gospel account actually opens with Jesus, who is thirsting and asks for a drink. The preface prayer for this Sunday refers to Jesus, who is thirsting for the Samaritan woman's faith.

Living Water

The second reading focuses on God's love which has been poured into our hearts through the action of the Holy Spirit and has been given to us as a gift even while we were sinners. The reference to "poured into our hearts" can clearly be interpreted as a baptismal reference.

Water figures prominently in the Hebrew Scriptures. The flood purified a sinful world. The Chosen people were delivered from bondage in Egypt by passing through walls of water. As they wandered through the desert, they were provided with manna, quail, and water from the rock to sustain them on their journey to the Promised Land. For a people who were not seagoing and who were uncomfortable with the thought of traveling over the murky depths, the mysterious sea was the home of the leviathan.

Water provides for life, but in its depths can be found death. This dual language is echoed in baptism, that fountain of living water where sinners die, only to rise with the Risen Christ to newness of life.

Jacob's Well

The site of the encounter between Jesus and the Samaritan woman is identified as Jacob's Well. It is the well where Jacob meets his future wife, Rachel. It is the well of love, of hope for the future, and of courtship. The exchange which takes place between Jesus and the Samaritan woman is not this type of courtship, and yet it is surely characterized by the offer of the gift of God's love and the hope for a firm future of authentic faith and worship. What is awakened in the Samaritan woman at the well of courtship is the "fountain within" that leaps up to provide eternal life.

The Hour

Several times in this gospel account, Jesus mentions either "the hour" or "an hour," a theme prevalent in the Gospel of John. *Hour* refers to the decisive moment of God's glory manifested in the death and resurrection of Jesus. This hour of glorification is impending, and functions as a backdrop to the conversation between Jesus and the woman. The ministry of Jesus is portrayed by the evangelist as leading up to this "hour." Those who encounter the Son of God as he journeys to that "hour" in John's Gospel either embrace or refuse his mission. The Samaritan woman and the whole town—ironically, heretics from the vantage point of temple worship—embrace Jesus and his mission.

God extends to us in Jesus the gift of living water, the life of faith. Jesus dies for us sinners and pours into our hearts the Spirit. This Spirit cannot be wholly contained, but by believers' words and deeds witness is made and the Good News is spread. From the well of encounter with the Lord to the marketplace of village, town, and city, the Word of love is deepened.

In this season, we who thirst are satisfied by worship in spirit and truth. Let us bow down and kneel before the Lord, who fashions us as a people of faith.

(Ordinarily this session will take thirty minutes.)

Getting Started

1. Gather in the space that has been prepared ahead of time that includes a large empty water jar.

2. Invite the elect and candidates to be seated. In silence, light the candle and then pray:

    Lord Jesus, you are the fountain for which we thirst,

    you are the water poured out on the parched earth,

    you are the healing river that renews the whole world.

    With this empty water jar we place our emptiness before you

    and ask you to fill us with water from the well that never runs dry.

3. Allow a few more moments of silence after the prayer.

Initial Reflection

1. Lead the elect and candidates in a reflection on the Liturgy of the Word and the Rite of Scrutiny that has just been celebrated, using this format or one of your own:

    Close your eyes and remember getting ready for church today. How were you feeling? . . . What were you thinking? . . . You arrived at church and met your godparent or your sponsor. (Hum or sing a little of the gathering song.)

    Father welcomed everyone and we prayed. The readings were proclaimed . . . The people grumbled against Moses . . . Why did you make us leave Egypt? . . . Is the Lord in our midst or not? . . . If today you hear God's voice, harden not your heart . . . While we were still sinners, Christ died for us. . . . Give me a drink . . . the well is deep . . . you have no bucket—living water welling up to provide eternal life. . . . Go, call your husband. . . .

    You are a prophet . . . worship in Spirit and Truth . . . food to eat of which you do not know . . . Come and see someone who told me everything . . . Many more came to believe in him. . . .

    Father invited us to pray . . . (Repeat some of the scrutiny intercessions.) Protect them . . . free them . . . hands were laid on your head . . . you are the Master whom they seek . . . confess their faults . . . heal them . . . rule over the spirit of evil . . . Go forth until the day you join us at the eucharistic table.

2. After several minutes of silence, invite them to speak a word or phrase that describes what they experienced. Allow for quiet moments after each person speaks.

3. Ask everyone to reflect on what the liturgy and Scrutiny proclaimed about God, about Jesus, and about grace. Discuss: What did it proclaim about the importance of a faith community gathering in prayer to ask for God's deliverance?

4. Invite everyone to share their reflection. Listen carefully and reflect back to the group some of their key words and phrases.

Prayer

Invite everyone to become silent. Sing or play "As Water to the Thirsty" (David Haas, GIA Publications Inc., 1987).

(Ordinarily this reflection will take sixty to ninety minutes.)

Processing

1. Welcome the godparents, sponsors, and team members as they arrive. After everyone is seated spend a brief time in silence and then sing an acclamation or song that has been part of today's Liturgy of the Word.

2. Give each person Handout 7 which has these questions for reflection:

   - The woman was freed and told the townspeople, "Come and see someone who told me everything I ever did." What parts of yourself that were hidden, not even admitted to you, have you now been freed to name for yourself and to Jesus?

   - The woman said, "Sir, you don't have a bucket." After she was freed, she put down her water jar. She did not need it because Jesus is living water. What are the things you hold on to, such as old attitudes, fears rather than receiving Jesus, who is living water? What ways or things do you need to let go of so that you might accept the living water which Jesus offers you?

   - How is Jesus living water for you? What are some of the means you have found helpful to find this living water who is Jesus?

   Give everyone fifteen to twenty minutes to silently pray and reflect on one of these questions. Tell them this might be difficult but stress the importance of taking the time to listen with the heart and to speak with God about their thoughts and reflections. Encourage them to ask God for what they desire and need.

3. Tell them when they are ready to share from their reflection to meet with their godparent or sponsor and pray for ten to fifteen minutes.

Putting Faith into Practice

1. Discuss the importance of praying daily for God's help to name what needs to change in our lives, in our communities, and in our society. Pray also for the courage to change from our old self to living as Christ taught us.

2. Based on their sharing, invite everyone to write an intercession. You might wish to give an example or two, such as:

   Jesus, you are the source of living water. In our empty lives, thirsting for . . . fill us with the living water of. . . .

   Or:

   We ask for the courage to change . . . so that we may draw water from the deep well of your compassion, Lord Jesus, and bring that water to the world parched by. . . .)

Prayer

Invite everyone to gather back together. After a few moments of quiet time, invite volunteers to pray aloud their intercessions. To each intercession have everyone respond, "Lord, hear our prayer" or a sung response. Conclude by singing an acclamation or song from today's Liturgy of the Word.

Third Sunday of Lent
Year B

The Cleansing of the Temple by Jesus

Exodus 20:1–17
Psalm 19:8, 11
1 Corinthians 1:22–25
John 2:13–25

There may be some years in the life of a parish when there are no elect, and the Period of Purification and Enlightenment is celebrated exclusively with baptized candidates for Confirmation and Eucharist and/or Reception into the full communion of the Catholic Church. During those years, the readings used for the Third, Fourth and Fifth Sunday of Lent do not revert to Year A, since the Scrutinies are not celebrated for the baptized candidates. However, because the period being celebrated is nevertheless one of purification and enlightenment, this background on the scripture readings and their images is offered.

Torah in Hebrew means "the ten words," which initially referred to the Ten Commandments but was later used to refer to the first five books of the Hebrew Scriptures, the Pentateuch, in which the Ten Commandments are enshrined. In today's scripture readings the Church reads from the passage in Exodus where the Ten Commandments are detailed. The Law given to Moses for the people of God to follow was considered the whole of the Pentateuch, whose heart is found in these Ten Commandments. This set of injunctions provided a rule or standard by which life was regulated and upon which individual, family, clan, and village relationships were established. The rule, as such, served the people of God well for hundreds and hundreds of years and it was not until much later that another body of oral interpretation arose which supplemented the Torah.

The "law of the LORD" that the psalmist extols is this rule by which life is regulated and guided—the decrees which are trustworthy and which impart wisdom that is sweeter than syrup or honey. The rabbis later came to use the metaphor of yoke for the Law (based on a figure of speech found in Jeremiah, chapter 28). This is what Jesus refers to elsewhere when he says, "take *my* yoke upon you . . . for my yoke is easy, and my burden light" (Matthew 11:29–30, NAB, author's emphasis).

Powerful figures of speech are found in this Sunday's gospel passage. Jesus, in cleansing the outer Temple precincts of money changers, refers to his own body as a "temple" which will be raised up in three days. This reference, at first misunderstood, is later recalled by the disciples after Jesus' resurrection from the dead. Just as Jesus himself, his teaching, preaching, and the whole of his mission fulfills the old Law and supercedes it with a new law, a new covenant, so too his body becomes the new temple of sacrifice, fulfilling all the sacrifices offered within the old Temple. As Paul writes to the Corinthian Christian community, the sign which is given and the wisdom imparted is found in "Christ crucified." That the God whom Christians worship died upon a cross is seen by some as a "stumbling block," a scandal, and an absurdity. For those who believe, however, it is the power of God and the font of wisdom.

IMAGES OF PURIFICATION AND ENLIGHTENMENT

Cleansing

That Jesus acted as he did was an attempt to purify the Temple precincts and call its users back to it as a place of prayer (see also Matthew 21:12–13, Mark 11:15–19, and Luke 19:45–48). However, the money-changing that took place in the outer courtyard was an activity that supported the Temple, in that every adult male nineteen years of age and older was required to pay an annual tax for its upkeep. Unlike the Synoptic accounts in which Jesus speaks of the Temple as a "house of prayer," John's account introduces the Temple as a metaphor for Jesus' own body.

Worship "cleanses" not by automatically engaging in routine ritual actions but in authentic prayer made holy by the sacrifice of Jesus. The body of Christ is the one true temple in which worship is constituted and rendered to God.

In His Name

Martyrs were called "confessors of the name" by the early Christian community. Names were considered by the ancient Hebrews as containing power for they were the way in which one was identified and called; and thus the way in which one responded to others. If one knew the name of another, one could claim the other; that is, call them.

In this gospel passage, John reports that because of the signs Jesus performed in Jerusalem "many believed in his name." When Moses asks for God's name on Sinai, God responds mysteriously, saying, "I am who am" and beyond this refuses to give his name. In the Gospel of John, God is presented as finally responding to that request. In Jesus' name, in his life, in his ministry, and especially in his saving death and resurrection, the name of God is revealed.

Ten Commandments

The Ten Commandments form the core upon which the whole of the Law, the Torah, is founded. They are considered the backbone of that whole body of commandments, statutes, and regulations that are expressed throughout the Pentateuch (but most notably in Deuteronomy and Leviticus). From the earliest times of interpretation of the Pentateuch, the Ten Commandments were described as the essential code, guiding the Chosen people in living out their covenant relationship with God.

Temple in Jerusalem

The Temple in Jerusalem was seen as the focus for worship of God. In Jesus' day, every male adult Jew was required to offer sacrifice at the Temple once a year. The Temple, as best as can be reconstructed from biblical descriptions, consisted of three main areas: the vestibule, the central courtyard, and the Holy of Holies. The general populace was not permitted to enter the Holy of Holies. The first Temple, Solomon's Temple, was destroyed by the Babylonians in 587 B.C. and the second, Herod the Great's Temple, was destroyed in A.D. 70.

When a Catholic church is dedicated, the preface prayer expresses the theme developed by Ephesians and Corinthians: The people of God, not a particular building, are being formed as the Body of Christ, a temple made of living stones, with Jesus himself as the capstone. "Through [Christ] the whole structure is fitted together and takes shape as a holy temple in the Lord; in him you are being built into this temple, to become a dwelling place for God in the Spirit" (Ephesians 2:21, NAB).

The Body of the Lord has been raised up. The Church is built, a temple not made with human hands. Sacrifice is rendered by the perfect offering of Christ.

Dedicate your house of prayer, O God, in the body of believers who gather and confess the power of Jesus' name who has saved us.

In this season, we celebrate the temple built of living stones and the Law of Good News that the Lord Jesus has planted deep within our hearts.

(Ordinarily this session will take thirty minutes.)

> *This session is used when there are no elect but only baptized candidates who will complete their Christian initiation or who will be received into the full communion of the Catholic Church.*

Getting Started

1. Gather everyone in the space that has been prepared ahead of time. Include a bowl of water.

2. Invite the candidates to be seated. Then have them close their eyes and take a few deep breaths.

3. Softly play music which contains sounds of water, such as the waves of the ocean, gentle rain, a thunderstorm, or a combination thereof. Pray in these or similar words:

   > *God of the wind and the water,*
   > *God of the lake and the ocean,*
   > *God of the river and the sea,*
   > *we give thanks and praise to you for the gift of life-sustaining water.*
   > *This wonderful gift of water which you so lavishly pour upon all creation was also poured upon each one of us as we were baptized into your family.*
   > *We ask you to bless us and to cleanse us with the blood of the Lamb, Jesus Christ, your Son, who so freely and lovingly gave his life for us so that we might be purified.*
   > *We ask this in his name, Jesus Christ, who is the living temple, now and forever. Amen.*

Initial Reflection

1. Invite the candidates to speak a word or phrase which struck them as significant in today's liturgy.

2. Ask them to reflect on the message they heard proclaimed in today's liturgy and on the ways that message challenges them to live out their baptismal promises.

3. After a few minutes of quiet time, invite them to share their reflections. Be attuned to such words and phrases as the importance of the Ten Commandments. Emphasize that God's ways are not our human ways and that God's "house" is not simply a building, but rather it is Christ, the living temple.

4. Summarize their reflections.

Prayer

Invite everyone to be quiet. Ask them to listen as you slowly and deliberately proclaim the threefold baptismal renunciations of Satan and sin and the threefold profession of faith. Invite everyone to come forward and touch the water in the bowl, and bless themselves, recalling their baptism.

(Ordinarily this session will take sixty to ninety minutes.)

Processing

1. Welcome the sponsors and other team members and ask them to be seated.

2. After a moment of silence ask everyone to close their eyes and take a few deep breaths.

3. Lead them in an imaginative reflection using these words or your own:

   Imagine that you are on your way home and all the road signs have been removed; or imagine that it's Monday and you arrive at work and no one knows the vision or goals of the business; or imagine your home in which everyone is living without rules; or imagine a world without rules. Picture the chaos. (Pause.) *What would it be like?*

   After they spend some time in quiet reflection, invite volunteers to describe out loud what life would be like without rules.

4. Proclaim the first reading, Exodus 20:1–17.

5. Invite the candidates to pair off with their sponsors and reflect and share using *one* of these questions:

   - In what ways are the Ten Commandments foundational to living the Christian life?

   - Which commandment is the easiest to keep and which commandment is the most difficult to keep? Why?

   - How do the Ten Commandments guide our relationship with God and our relationship with one another?

6. After twenty minutes or so, ask everyone to come back together. Invite them to share the insights they gained from their reflection and sharing.

7. Involve everyone in a conversation about how the Ten Commandments relate to our baptismal promises and the struggle between good and evil in which all of us are engaged. Explore ways in which the Ten Commandments guide us to live our baptismal promises.

Putting Faith into Practice

1. Ask everyone to think about the rules they use to make decisions at work, at home, and in society in general. Then ask them to discuss how these rules reflect or do not reflect the Ten Commandments and our baptismal promises.

2. Stress that the Lenten scripture readings, in particular, offer us an opportunity to examine how we are living our lives and to discern what is of God, what needs to be strengthened, and what is sinful in our life and needs to be amended.

3. Encourage everyone to spend some time this week prayerfully examining their lives in light of the commandments.

Prayer

After everyone has become quiet, sing or listen to "Deep Within" (David Haas, GIA Publications, Inc., 1987) or another appropriate hymn. Invite everyone to come to the water as they leave and to bless one another.

Third Sunday of Lent
Year C

The Parable of the Fig Tree

Exodus 3:1–8, 13–15
Psalm 103:1–4, 6–8, 11
1 Corinthians 10:1–6, 12
Luke 13:1–9

There may be some years in the life of a parish when there are no elect, and the Period of Purification and Enlightenment is celebrated exclusively with baptized candidates preparing for Confirmation and Eucharist and/or Reception into the full communion of the Catholic Church. During those years, the readings used for the Third, Fourth and Fifth Sunday of Lent do not revert to Year A, since the Scrutinies are not celebrated for the baptized candidates. However, because the period being celebrated is nevertheless one of purification and enlightenment, this background on the Scripture readings and their images is offered.

Moses, investigating the phenomenon of the burning bush which is not consumed, hears the call of God. When he asks the name of God, so that he may make proper representation to the Israelites in Egypt, the divine voice answers "I am who am." One interpretation of this response is that God will not tell Moses his name, for in those days it was believed that knowing someone's name gave power over that person. However, another interpretation of this mysterious response suggests that if "I am who am" is transposed into the third person required by the causative, Yahweh, it reads *Yahweh asher yihweh*, that is, "He causes to be what comes into existence" (W. F. Albright and Patricia Datchuck Sanchez, *The Word We Celebrate*, Sheed & Ward, 1989, p. 287–88). The God who calls Moses is the God who creates,

who causes, who will rescue the people and bring them up out of slavery into "a good and spacious land, a land flowing with milk and honey." This interpretation works well, especially when read in the context of Moses' call, for "He causes to be what comes into existence" has caused Israel to be and it reminds Moses of that truth by referring to the forebears and patriarchs—Abraham, Isaac, and Jacob. As the responsorial psalm for this liturgy expresses, God's ways are made known to Moses and his deeds to the children of Israel. God has acted to create Israel and God will continue to act to deliver them with deeds of power and love.

In the gospel passage from Luke, Jesus refers both to a despicable act by Pilate (apparently a massacre or execution of some Galileans) and a tragic event (a tower which fell and crushed eighteen people) to impress upon his listeners the urgency of reform and repentance. In those days many people believed that such tragedies were divine punishment for sin. Jesus uses the occasion to teach that everyone has been given a limited amount of time by the grace of God, and he urges everyone to reform.

The parable of the fig tree underscores Jesus' message. Fig trees were expected to produce fruit after the third year that they were planted. If they did not, they were cut down and others were planted in their place. The owner in the parable is unusually generous and allows the fig tree in his vineyard not three years but four. It is cared for, hoed, and manured so that it might bear fruit. But the warning is there. If after the fourth year of this special caring it does not produce fruit, it will be cut down. The call to reform is clear in this passage. God gives us a chance—care is lavished upon the vineyard. Those who follow Jesus must reform their lives and bear fruit.

The second reading emphasizes this same message. The events of salvation history are a clear warning and an example. The message is there for those who discern it—and thereby benefit from it. God has acted in the past and is definitely acting now in Jesus to save the world. In the light of this divine care and loving kindness, reform is the required response.

IMAGES OF PURIFICATION AND ENLIGHTENMENT

Kind and Merciful

God initiates, God takes the first action in creating a people. Throughout the long story of God's relationship with Israel and whenever they wander away from the covenant, God always brings them back. Today's psalm exults in the kindness and mercy of the Most High. God is portrayed as "slow to anger and abounding in kindness."

This overwhelming graciousness is most fully revealed in Jesus, whose name literally means "God saves." Such an immense gift requires a response: lives which are reformed according to God's ways. The first step in such a response is given by the psalmist: "Bless the LORD, O my soul, and all that is within me, bless his holy name."

The Fig Tree

In the Hebrew Scriptures, the fig tree symbolizes Israel, the people of God. This image is especially evident in the prophets (Hosea 9:10, Micah 7:1, Jeremiah 8:13). So, too, is the vine and vineyard an image of Israel (Numbers 13:20–26; Isaiah 27:2–5, Psalm 79:9–10).

These farming images speak vividly of fruitfulness, of the miracle of growth, of patient care, tillage, watering, and protecting. Fig trees, vines, and vineyards do not produce without proper care and protection. These are precisely what God offered in the covenant established with Israel and in his Son, Jesus.

God's mighty hand calls us out of slavery to sin and promises us a land overflowing with milk and honey, an abundant kingdom of grace. The deeds of God's loving kindness sow within us seeds of repentance. Now is the time to turn from sin. Now is the time to produce fruit with lives of holiness and goodness.

In this season, we celebrate the God who cares for us, saves us, and reforms us.

(Ordinarily this session will take thirty minutes.)

This session is used when there are no elect but only baptized candidates who will complete their Christian initiation or who will be received into the full communion of the Catholic Church.

Getting Started

1. Gather everyone into the space that has been prepared ahead of time. Light the candle and pray in these or similar words:

   O Merciful God, you have given us the greatest gift, Jesus, the One who saves.
   Thank you for your unconditional love and never-ending mercy.
   Help us to be strong in the face of temptation. Strengthen our resolve to be faithful to the covenant which you have established with us.
   We ask this in the name of Jesus, our brother, who lives and reigns with you and the Holy Spirit one God forever and ever. Amen.

   Sing "The Lord is Kind and Merciful" (Marty Haugen, GIA Publications, Inc., 1993).

Initial Reflection

1. Recall with the candidates words, phrases, and feelings experienced in the Liturgy of the Word today.

2. Reflect with them on the responsorial psalm, in particular the words "Merciful and gracious is the LORD, / slow to anger, abounding in kindness" (Ps 103:8, NAB). Slowly read through the verses of Psalm 103, pausing to allow time for thoughts, feelings, and images to emerge within the candidates.

3. Ask them to describe the image of God that the psalmist portrays.

4. Allow time for them to create their own verses to add to this psalm. Tell them not to worry about rhyme or length.

Prayer

Invite everyone to gather back together. After a few moments of quiet time, lead them in singing the refrain "The Lord is Kind and Merciful." Then ask several candidates to pray aloud the psalm verse which they have written. Sing the refrain after each verse is prayed. Continue this pattern until all who wish have had the opportunity to pray their verse.

(Ordinarily this session will take sixty to ninety minutes.)

Processing

1. Welcome the sponsors and other team members. After everyone has been seated, proclaim the Gospel.

2. Invite everyone to spend some quiet time alone, pondering *one* of these questions:

   - What in your life is in need of the repentance or reform that Jesus speaks about?

   - What keeps you from fully embracing the covenant and the call to discipleship that baptism establishes?

   - What keeps you from accepting God's loving mercy?

   - What in your life needs to change?

3. After fifteen to twenty minutes, encourage the candidates and their sponsors to get together and share their personal reflection. Remind everyone that they are the gatekeepers of their own experiences and they are free to choose how much they want to share with each other.

4. After fifteen to twenty minutes ask everyone to come back together. Invite them to share what affirmations, insights, or challenges they gained from their reflection and sharing.

5. Explore the gospel image of the fig tree. Ask everyone to think about the "throw-away" mentality that many people have and to discuss in what ways such a mentality, which is similar to the fig tree in the gospel reading, doesn't produce fruit and deserves simply to be pulled up and tossed into the fire. Ponder what it would be like if God treated us in the same way. Yet our God is faithful, generous, and forgiving, no matter what we say or do or what we fail to say or do.

6. Ask the candidates and their sponsors to name and discuss together ways to live lives which produce holiness and goodness. After five minutes or so, collect their suggestions.

Putting Faith into Practice

1. With the group, reflect on the challenge to live faith-filled lives. Stress that God does not simply focus on our triumphs; God is interested in our struggles to produce—to be faithful to our baptismal commitment and to live as followers of Jesus Christ.

2. Encourage everyone to take time each day to briefly examine their conscience by naming what happened during the day, for which they want to give thanks to God and for which they want to ask for forgiveness, and by naming what strengthened them to live their commitment to follow Jesus.

Prayer

Invite everyone to stand. Pray in these or similar words:

> *O God, your mighty hand called us out of slavery and led us to the promised land overflowing with your abundant grace.*
> *Help us repent and change our lives.*
> *Now is the time for us to produce the fruit of holiness and goodness. We celebrate you, God, for you care for us. You save us and you reform us. Amen.*

Sing again "The Lord is Kind and Merciful" by Marty Haugen or another appropriate refrain.

Fourth Sunday of Lent
Year A

The Man Born Blind

1 Samuel 16:1, 6–7, 10–13
Psalm 23:1–6
Ephesians 5:8–14
John 9:1–41

When the second Scrutiny is celebrated, the readings are always taken from Year A (Lectionary, 746). While the central imagery of this set of readings revolves around enlightenment, seeing, light and darkness, there is also a strong baptismal theme running through the second reading and the gospel passage.

In the first reading, God is portrayed as clearly being in control of the situation—choosing "the youngest," the least among Jesse's sons as heaven's anointed to replace Saul. While David is formally identified as king later in the narrative, he is introduced here; and the ritual sign of anointing is performed by the prophet to indicate God's choice. Even though David had not been originally presented to Samuel along with the other, older sons, the spirit of the Lord rushes in and claims this lowly youngster who had been shepherding the sheep. The key to understanding what transpires is contained in the line "the Lord looks on the heart," that is, God looks beneath outward appearances and judges the true worth of an individual, unlike humans who frequently misjudge others because they rely on externals. God sees, in other words, from the inside out.

The very last part of the reading from Ephesians, which is a portion from an ancient baptismal hymn, applies the theme of enlightenment and waking from sleep to this initiation sacrament. Darkness provides a cover for sinful activities, but the light of Christ exposes shameful deeds. In that enlightenment the believer awakes to the life of grace as a child of God. There is a connection with the first reading from Ephesians in the line "Be correct in your judgment of what pleases the Lord (Eph 5:10)." Such an appraisal depends on the enlightenment that Christ offers: Those who walked in dark valleys (Psalm 23) are being shepherded by God in Christ to live as children of the light and so have nothing to fear. Early Christians described baptism as "enlightenment" or "illumination."

The gospel passage contains John's entire ninth chapter, which details the sixth sign or miracle of Jesus in John's Gospel. It is the account of the man who was born sightless and is given sight by Jesus while the religious authorities, who are born seeing, question this miracle, doubt Jesus, and are labeled as "blind." In this chapter, physical sight is employed as a metaphor for spiritual insight and understanding. The man who has been cured gradually acknowledges the true identity of Jesus, the light of the world, first calling Jesus "that man" (verse ll); second, "prophet" (verse 17); third, "man from God" (verse 33); and finally, at the climax, "Son of Man" and "Lord" or in Greek *kyrios* (verse 38), when he bows down to Jesus in worship.

In his encounter with Jesus the man grows in faith. The critics of Jesus, on the other hand, are initially concerned that he has broken a sabbath law by performing work (making the mud paste and smearing it on the man's eyes). And as they question the man himself and his parents, they refuse to believe that the miracle that has occurred is the action of God among them. Thus, they remain in the dark. This sign of Jesus in the Gospel of John points to Jesus as the One sent by God to be the light of the world, who makes the sightless see and the supposedly seeing, blind.

IMAGES OF PURIFICATION AND ENLIGHTENMENT

Sent by God

The man who is cured of his blindness in the gospel passage receives his sight after washing in the Pool of Siloam. The name of this place, Siloam, is similar to the Hebrew word *shalah,* which means "sent." Clearly, the evangelist means to draw a connection to the earlier reference to Jesus in the Gospel to Jesus as the One sent by God (John 3:17) who comes not to condemn the world but to save it. To prompt the washing, the blind man is anointed by Jesus. Early Christian communities used this gospel passage in celebrating baptismal liturgies, and the art of the catacombs depicts this anointing of the man blind from birth. But who is the One truly being sent and the One anointed? Jesus, the Son of God, is the One sent and anointed; Christ, given for our salvation, is the One to whom we are joined in baptism. Thus, we too are washed, anointed, and sent forth on a mission with Christ.

Blindness/Sight

Today's gospel passage opens with a question put to Jesus by the disciples, who ask what caused the blindness of the beggar. In Jesus' day many believed that sickness was a punishment from God for sin, whether it was one's own sin or the sin of one's forebearers. Jesus teaches otherwise. Sickness and debilitation are not punishments meted out to sinners by God. The physical blindness of the man, moreover, becomes the occasion for the glory of God to shine forth through the action of Jesus. A cure is effected on the physical level, but a deeper "cure" takes place as the man "sees" that Jesus is truly the Son of God and the Light of the world.

Those who question this miracle and doubt its goodness are versed in the Law and the Prophets. They are considered religious leaders. Because of their knowledge and status, they should "see" what is taking place. Yet they are so blind in their ways that they cannot "see" that the Light has come into the world. They remain in darkness, blind to the sign in front of their very eyes.

Recognition

In the first reading, David, who was not even considered for presentation to the prophet, is chosen by God to lead Israel, and in his anointing he is recognized as king. In the second reading, the enlightenment of baptism enables one to recognize "goodness, justice and truth" and to walk in the ways of life. Walking as a child of the light equips one to recognize evil deeds done in darkness, to identify these ways of death, and to oppose them. In the gospel passage, the man who is cured of his blindness eventually recognizes who Jesus is and worships him as Lord.

God shepherds us through the dark valley and provides for us, anointing us with overflowing life. We have been raised up by God, who chooses to accompany us in goodness and kindness.

As children of the light who walk in the ways of life, we are awakened from sleep by the waters of baptism and in Christ are called to faith. We see in the Lord—the Son, the Morning Star, the Sun—whose rays of grace illumine our minds and hearts and who gives us the grace of true sight.

(Ordinarily this session will take thirty minutes.)

Getting Started

1. Gather everyone into the space that has been prepared ahead of time. Invite the elect and candidates to be seated in pairs.

2. After a moment of silence, light the candle and lead everyone in singing a song or acclamation from the Liturgy of the Word that has just been celebrated.

Initial Reflection

1. Ask the elect and candidates to reflect on the Liturgy of the Word and the Rite of Scrutiny that has just been celebrated. After several minutes of silence, invite them to share a word or phrase that describes what they experienced in the celebration. Allow for a moment of quiet after each person speaks.

2. Invite participants to close their eyes. Say in these or similar words:

   Recall what you experienced and felt during the Rite of Scrutiny. *You elect were invited to kneel in the midst of the community of the faithful. The community was asked to pray for and with you. The* Litany of Intercession *was prayed, turning all that is sinful over to the power of Christ. After the quiet settled, we all prayed, calling on God to free you. Hands were laid on your head in deep silence. Another powerful prayer was prayed with hands extended over you. You were sent forth. When you are ready, open your eyes and come back to this space.*

3. Ask the participants to share with the person next to them one or two things from the Scrutiny that touched them and stands out in their memory. Allow time for this sharing. Then ask each pair to share with the entire group what touched them. (Note: At times this Scrutiny has a very powerful impact on participants. Continue to stay with their experience and feelings as long as they have something to share.)

4. Ask the members of the entire group to reflect on what they experienced as God's further invitation to them as a result of their participation in the Rite of Scrutiny. After several minutes, ask the group to name words or phrases that summarize their sharing. Listen attentively and reflect back to the group some of their key insights.

Prayer

Invite everyone to share in a moment of quiet time. Turn off the lights so that the focus is on the light of the candle. Sing "Amazing Grace."

(Ordinarily this session will take sixty to ninety minutes.)

Processing

1. Welcome the godparents, sponsors, and team members as they arrive. Invite the godparents and sponsors to be seated with their elect or candidate. Ask for a few moments of silence, and then sing a song or acclamation that has been part of the Liturgy of the Word.

2. Give each person Handout 10 which provides an opportunity to reflect and discuss the following:

   - All of the characters in the gospel story have traits found in each of us: the blind man to whom Jesus gave sight, the pharisees who questioned Jesus' actions and were concerned about laws and rules, the parents who really didn't want to get too involved. *What is the new sight or vision Jesus is offering to you? Is there a part of you—some excuse, belief, feeling, or rationalization—that resists?*

   - The blind man received sight. He was open to Jesus. Jesus offered him more than physical sight. *How are your eyes being opened to see in a new way who Jesus is for you?*

   - *What is the message of the closing dialogue between Jesus and the Pharisees concerning seeing, blindness, and sin? What are the implications of this dialogue for us, who call ourselves believers?*

3. Invite everyone to take fifteen to twenty minutes to listen to, reflect on, and pray about *one* of the above. Then ask them to take time to speak with Jesus about their thoughts and reflections and what they desire, or need, in order to see with the eyes of faith.

4. When they are ready, ask the participants to join with their godparents or sponsors to share what they gained from their insights, challenges, and thoughts. Allow at least fifteen minutes for this sharing before inviting them to come back together and sit, forming a circle.

5. Gather any responses from the reflection that they wish to share. Listen attentively and affirm and/or restate their insights about blindness and seeing, darkness and light, and Jesus as the Light of the world.

Putting Faith into Practice

1. Encourage everyone to converse with God throughout their day, in particular when they are experiencing a challenge to living as a Christian. Also encourage them to thank God for the blessings of each day.

2. Ask them to name the ways in which Jesus is the light for them.

3. Reflect with them on the gift of Jesus as the Light of the world.

Prayer

Invite everyone to become quiet. After a brief moment of quiet time, ask them to think about how they would complete this petition:

> *Lord Jesus, I bring you my blindness of . . .* (Pause.) *Heal me, and give me your true sight.*

Invite anyone who wishes to pray their petition aloud. After all have had the opportunity to pray, lead everyone in singing the first and last verses of "Amazing Grace."

Fourth Sunday of Lent
Year B

Nicodemus' Encounter with Jesus

2 Chronicles 36:14–17, 19–23
Psalm 137:1–6
Ephesians 2:4–10
John 3:14–21

There may be some years in the life of a parish when there are no elect, and the Period of Purification and Enlightenment is celebrated exclusively with baptized candidates preparing for Confirmation and Eucharist and/or for Reception into the full communion of the Catholic Church. During those years, the readings used for the Third, Fourth and Fifth Sunday of Lent do not revert to Year A, since the Scrutinies are not celebrated for the baptized candidates. However, because the period being celebrated is nevertheless one of purification and enlightenment, this background on the Scripture readings and their images is offered.

The contrast between the tone of the first reading and the gospel passage could not be greater. The passage from 2 Chronicles presents an image of a vengeful God who in divine justice passes judgment upon the people who have failed to keep the covenant, gone against the Law, and "added infidelity to infidelity, practicing all the abominations . . . and polluting the Lord's temple." In the gospel account of Nicodemus' encounter with Jesus, God is presented as loving and saving. It would be wrong, however, to interpret this contrast as presenting God as One who changes in relating to humanity.

God's judgment is the same in every age. In the gospel passage, it is not that God is any less of a judge, but simply that the perspective of the

Scriptures has changed from the viewpoint of God presented in 2 Chronicles to the experience and reality of humanity presented in the evangelist's narrative. The judgment of God still operates in John's account; but it is presented as a judgment which takes place automatically because of one's actions: A person is already judged by the way one lives or fails to live faith, by the way one accepts or rejects Jesus Christ, the Light of the world. In the fourth Gospel, people encounter Jesus, and they either rise to the light in faith or they sink into the faithless darkness, unable to accept God's Anointed One, Christ.

God's love is also the same in every age. The difference, however, between the time of the king of the Chaldeans (first reading), who destroyed the Temple and the people for infidelity, and the time of Nicodemus (gospel reading), is the presence of the person of Jesus Christ, who embodied the love of God. Divine salvation is made manifest in the Master from Nazareth who will, in the climax of his mission, be "lifted up" on the cross so that all can see the extent of God's love. Condemnation comes from one's own response to this lifting up. The message is clear for all to see and embrace. It is a matter of our responding.

IMAGES OF PURIFICATION AND ENLIGHTENMENT

Babylon

The very first scriptural reference to Babylon is implied in Genesis in the description of the "tower of Babel," when people thought they could reach heaven through their own means by erecting a massive edifice that went "nowhere." The outcome of the story of the tower of Babel is chaos, as in *babble,* and the roots of this chaos are found in the self-defeating, overwhelming pride of people.

It was the Babylonian Empire that conquered the Israelites and sent the people into exile. The remnant, or survivors, of God's people saw in those disastrous events of the Exile the effects of divine judgment and wrath against the nation for its infidelity and worship of idols. "By the rivers of Babylon" the people sat and added their tears to the waters, says the psalm for today. There were no songs; for how could God's people, bereft of the Promised Land, sing? The only songs were sounds from the rivers of judgment.

Rich in Mercy

The Scriptures again and again tell of the loving kindness of God, but the people forget. They lose sight, they lack wisdom, they turn to other foreign gods and idols. But God does not forget, and God does not stop loving them. God faithfully seeks out and brings back those who wander. Paul exclaims to the Ephesians that God is "rich in mercy."

Rich in Mercy is the title of a papal encyclical, and its guiding scriptural image is taken from the narrative in John's Gospel in which Jesus says that those who see the Son see the Father (14:9). As Paul writes in his letter to the Ephesians, "the great wealth of [God's] favor" is shown to us in Christ Jesus.

Deeds Done in the Dark/ Deeds Done in the Light

Scripture asserts that faith necessarily includes doing, acting. John's Gospel divides actions into the categories of those done in the dark and those done in the light. Those who faithfully follow Jesus have nothing to hide, while those who love evil seek out the shadows and darkness, for their actions must be concealed.

Deeds of light are done in God and therefore are "shouted from the rooftops," for they are good news. Lamps are not covered by bushel baskets to hide their light but are placed on lampstands to give light to all in the house (Matthew 5:15, NAB).

We are lifted up in Jesus to revel in deeds done in the light, to share in the richness of God's eternal mercy. Love takes flesh in Christ and the handiwork of God is accomplished in those who embrace the Light of the world, a light no darkness can extinguish.

In this season of the church year, we celebrate the place in heaven that is our inheritance as brothers and sisters of the One who has come into the world, not to condemn it, but that the world might have life, life to the fullest.

(Ordinarily this session will take thirty minutes.)

> *This session is used when there are no elect but only baptized candidates to complete their Christian initiation or to be received into the full communion of the Catholic Church.*

Getting Started

1. Gather everyone into the space that has been prepared ahead of time. Place enough tapers on the table for each person present to use at the end of the session.

2. Ask everyone to be seated. Light the candle and invite everyone to speak to the Lord in the quiet of their hearts.

3. After several minutes, invite the group to sing a song or acclamation from the Liturgy of the Word that has just been celebrated or to sing "Shepherd Me, O God" (Marty Haugen, GIA Publications, Inc., 1986).

Initial Reflection

1. Ask everyone to close their eyes, take a few deep breaths, and recall the Liturgy of the Word that has just been celebrated. Invite them to share a feeling, mood, word, or phrase from today's liturgy that moved them.

2. Invite them to reflect on the image of God's abundant love and mercy found in Paul's Letter to the Ephesians.

3. Ask them to share with one other person a time when they have experienced God's abounding love and mercy.

4. With the entire group name many of the ways we, children of God, experience this outpouring of love and mercy.

Prayer

Conclude with a prayer using these or similar words:

> *God, you are rich in mercy.*
> *Your words and deeds are precious to us.*
> *You love us so much that you gave us your Son to bring us to light and goodness.*
> *Help us keep our eyes focused on you.*
> *Give us the grace to believe more deeply in Jesus and in the life he offers us.*
> *Make us people of the light.*
> *Surround us and fill us with your light.*
> *Hear our prayer that we pray with love and trust. Amen.*

(Ordinarily this session will take sixty to ninety minutes.)

Processing

1. Welcome sponsors and other team members. Invite everyone to be seated.

2. Proclaim the Gospel.

3. After a few moments of quiet time, pair candidates and sponsors and give each pair a sheet of paper on which the two headings, "Deeds Done in Darkness" and "Deeds Done in Light" have been written. Ask each pair to list wicked deeds that people do not want brought to the light (cheating, exploitation, racial injustices, and so on), and good deeds done in the light (sheltering the homeless, feeding the hungry, recycling, and so on).

4. As they finish, invite them to continue working in pairs and discuss the ways they participate in the deeds of darkness and the deeds of light.

5. After fifteen to twenty minutes, call everyone to come back together. Invite them to name insights, affirmations, and challenges they gained from their conversations.

6. Ask them to reflect quietly on the following:

   How easy it is to blame someone or some organization for the deeds of darkness in which we participate. Yet, each of us has a free will. We can choose to do or not to do that which weakens our relationship with God and with our communities. God's mercy is available for those who recognize their need for forgiveness. Jesus has already died and is risen for us. God's grace is abundant and free for the asking.

7. Conclude with ten minutes of silent reflection.

Putting Faith into Practice

1. Encourage participants to journal for a few minutes about the challenges they experience in their efforts to live in light rather than in darkness.

2. Lead them in naming what needs to change in their own lives and in the life of the community in order to walk as children of light. Lead them also in naming the ways in which Jesus Christ is the Light of the world.

Prayer

Hand a taper to everyone present. Turn off all lights and ask everyone to focus on the lighted candle on the table. Speak softly about the candle as a source of light that shines for all but in doing so is consumed. Call each one by name, inviting the person to come and light their taper from the lighted candle. After all arc holding lighted candles, join in singing or listening to "We Walk By Faith" (Marty Haugen, GIA Publications, Inc., 1984).

Fourth Sunday of Lent
Year C

The Parable of the Prodigal Son

Joshua 5:9, 10–12
Psalm 34:2–7
2 Corinthians 5:17–21
Luke 15:1–3, 11–32

There may be some years in the life of a parish when there are no elect, and the Period of Purification and Enlightenment is celebrated exclusively with baptized candidates preparing for Confirmation and Eucharist and/or Reception into the full communion of the Catholic Church. During those years, the readings used for the Third, Fourth and Fifth Sunday of Lent do not revert to Year A, since the Scrutinies are not celebrated for the baptized candidates. However, because the period being celebrated is nevertheless one of purification and enlightenment, this background on the Scriptures and their images is offered.

The first reading recounts the initial Passover celebration held in the Promised Land. The people of God have ended their long journey and are now settling upon the land given to them. Wandering in the wilderness will become a memory; and a settled, relatively secure life will become a reality. The manna stops and they begin to partake of the goodness of a fruitful land. The Passover functions as a reminder of their deliverance at the hand of God, who freed them from slavery and enjoined upon them a covenant for all time, whether wandering or settled.

Today's gospel parable revolves around the wanderings of two sons, the younger who takes his inheritance and squanders it and the older who angrily confronts his father over the joyous reconciliation extended to his younger wayward brother who has returned. The parable's focus is the father's loving response to both sons. Jesus presents the parable because some of the religious leaders criticized him not only for associating with unclean and impure sinners but also for eating with them. This story is meant as a lesson in God's reconciling grace.

The younger son leaves everything behind and squanders his inheritance. He falls so deeply into need that he forsakes the religious traditions of his people and "takes care of the pigs," unclean animals. He would even eat their fodder if he could. In this dire, despicable condition, he realizes how far he has fallen and resolves to return. The action of the father is instructive and amazing. The father does not act sternly, reproaching the younger son (as well he might) for his tremendous folly. Rather, in loving kindness the father runs to him, embracing and kissing him, welcoming him back into the household. Despite the fact that the son had taken all of his legally allotted inheritance—nothing more of the father's was his to claim—but the father does not treat him as a hireling or a slave but gives him gifts of a robe, a ring, shoes, and an extravagant celebration (meat was eaten rarely).

The older son, who has not run off with and squandered his share of the inheritance but has faithfully toiled for his father, is angry and confronts him with what he sees as an injustice. The father responds that "all that is mine is yours." Both sons receive the father's love. Some commentators have termed this story the parable of the *prodigal father* in virtue of the prodigious love which the father shows to both sons.

As Jesus presents it, the parable is a lesson on how God relates to all sinners, extending divine love to them even while they are still sinners. This astounding gift makes possible one's repentance.

"Taste and see that the Lord is good" is the psalm refrain for today's liturgy. Indeed, celebration and joy characterize the readings for this Sunday, for God has loved us while we were still sinners. Because of that love, Paul preaches, "everything old has passed away." By the mission and ministry of Jesus, God reconciles all to the household of believers and the celebration begins.

IMAGES OF PURIFICATION AND ENLIGHTENMENT

Ambassadors for Christ

Paul applies the image of "ambassadors of Christ" to his own ministry as preacher and apostle. All those, however, who have tasted the goodness of the Lord and experienced his reconciling love are ambassadors empowered to share this good news with others.

The gift given is shared with others, just as Jesus taught his disciples in prayer, "forgive us our debts, / as we forgive our debtors" (Matthew 6:12, NAB). By holy lives, the people of God become ambassadors for Christ, who reconciles us to the Father.

Lost/Found

Twice in this gospel parable the father states that the younger son had been lost but now found, had been dead but now brought back to life (verses 24 and 32). The image of that which was lost and is now found appears elsewhere in the gospel accounts (the lost coin, the lost sheep). In each instance, joy is the response in finding that which was lost.

For all the intensity of purpose that surrounds the season of Lent and this time of purification and enlightenment—with such a strong emphasis on reconciliation, turning from sin, and confronting evil—there is, nonetheless, a theme of *joy* which permeates this time in the liturgical year and final stage of proximate preparation for initiation. It is the joy of conversion, of once being lost and now being found in Jesus Christ.

Father and Son

Few relationships in life are so rich and complex as those which exist between parents and children. Love, loyalty, deep identifications, fears, conflicts, and hopes are all alluded to in the parable of the prodigal son, which deftly uses the character of the loving father and his two sons to reveal a profound divine truth in human terms.

In the ancient Mediterranean world, both before and during the time of Jesus, few relationships in family and society were so privileged as that between father and son. The father was the head of the household and of the extended family, the clan, or tribe. One's honor and identity derived from one's father. To know the father was to know the son. (Jesus called God, his father, "Abba," an intimate term pointing to a relationship of trust, obedience, and affection.) Because a father gave life to his children, a father's sons were always in his debt. To squander an inheritance was an act of great disrespect, bringing shame upon son and father alike. In the parable, the father's astonishing act of mercy, however, is capable of restoring honor to his disgraced son and reincorporating him into the family.

Honor and identity, however, are not the only dimensions of the relationship between the father and son that concerns the parable treats. The father and son also share bonds of life and love. The elder son's outwardly respectable relationship to the father is exposed by the parable to be inwardly and deeply flawed as the elder son bitterly resents the father's love for his wayward brother and complains of his own lot, protesting he has slaved for the father with no recompense. The parable assures us of the father's love for his elder son, but the ultimate fate of that son's relationship with his father is left as an unanswered question for the hearer to ponder.

The God who loves us does not hold back but runs to us with the robe and ring and sandals of reconciliation. Sinners once lost are now found in Christ. Taste and see the goodness of the Lord!

In this season of the liturgical year, we celebrate with joy the newness of life we have been given in Jesus Christ.

(Ordinarily this session will take thirty minutes.)

> *This session is used when there are no elect but only baptized candidates to complete their Christian initiation or to be received into full communion of the Catholic Church.*

Getting Started

1. Gather everyone into the space that has been prepared ahead of time. Display a large loaf of bread.

2. Invite everyone to be seated and then light the candle. Pray in these or similar words:

   Loving God, you hold each person in the palm of your hand.
   Your love is so unconditional;
   your desire to be united with everyone is so strong.
   Help us to trust in your undying love
   and to know that no matter how far we may stray, you are waiting with open hands to welcome us home.
   We ask this in the name of Jesus Christ, our brother, who lives and reigns with you and the Holy Spirit, one God, forever and ever. Amen.

Initial Reflection

1. Ask the candidates to take a few deep breaths and to recall and reflect on the Liturgy of the Word that was just celebrated. Invite them to share a feeling or mood, a word or phrase from today's Liturgy that particularly moved them.

2. Invite the candidates to recall a time of forgiveness, saying:

   Close your eyes. Recall a time in your life when forgiveness was offered to you before you even asked for it. (Pause.)
   What was the occasion? (Pause.)
   Who was involved? (Pause.)
   How did you respond to the offer of forgiveness? (Pause.)
   How did such an offer make you feel? (Pause.)

3. After a few minutes of quiet reflection, invite them to share their thoughts in pairs. Allow about ten minutes.

4. Ask all the candidates to come back together. Elicit any responses they might want to share with the whole group.

Prayer

Use Psalm 34, "Taste and See," from today's liturgy.

(Ordinarily this session will take sixty to ninety minutes.)

Processing

1. Welcome the sponsors and other team members. After everyone has been seated, invite them to listen to today's proclamation of the Gospel.

2. Give everyone Handout 12 that contains the following questions:

   • When in your life have you been the prodigal son, squandering your possessions, time, or talents on things that do not matter?

   • When in your life have you been the older son, angry that the sinner has been so easily forgiven, wanting the sinner to be punished severely for the sins, perhaps never receiving forgiveness?

   • When in your life have you been the father, wanting to offer forgiveness to another so much that you offer it even before the other can say "I'm sorry"?

   • What does this gospel parable tell you about God? About Jesus Christ, who loves you so much that before you were born he died for you?

3. Encourage everyone to find a quiet place and to privately ponder the above questions for fifteen to twenty minutes. Explain that when they are ready, sponsors and candidates are to find each other and share the outcome of their reflections. Allow an additional ten to fifteen minutes for their sharing.

4. Gather the group back together, inviting volunteers to share the fruit of their reflection and sharing. Be attuned to what they say. When everyone has finished sharing, give a brief summary for the whole group, including the fact that at various times we take on the role of each character in the parable.

5. Invite the group to name what this parable tells us about God, about Jesus Christ, about their own desire to offer us forgiveness. Summarize their statements.

Putting Faith into Practice

Encourage everyone to spend time this week reflecting on each of the following questions:

   • How do I forgive others?

   • How do I ask for and receive forgiveness?

   • What are the occasions when I refuse to accept or give forgiveness at home? In the workplace? In the community?

Prayer

Take the loaf of bread in your hands and say in these or similar words:

> *Today we heard the parable of a father who throws a big feast for his son who was lost. Our God invites us to share fully in the meal of the Eucharist where we are all one, sinners and saints alike. Just as our God provided manna in the desert for the Israelites, so, too, our God provides us food for the journey. I invite you to break a piece of bread from this loaf as a sign that we all are called to share in the banquet of God's love.*

Join in singing "Remember Your Love" (Daryl Ducote and Gary Daigle, Damean Music, distributed by GIA Publications, Inc., 1978).

Fifth Sunday of Lent
Year A

The Raising of Lazarus

Ezekiel 37:12–14
Psalm 130: 1–8
Romans 8:8–11
John 11:1–45

When the third Scrutiny is celebrated, the readings are always taken from Year A (Lectionary, 747). Seen through the lens of the gospel text, this set of readings clearly revolves around the theme of Jesus, who is "the resurrection and the life" (John 11:25).

As the story of Jesus unfolds in the Gospel of John, these events at Bethany are pivotal. Jesus raises Lazarus from death and the grave. The evangelist presents the religious leaders as deeply threatened by this action and are thus prompted to move decisively against Jesus. Ironically, the gift of life given to Lazarus by Jesus leads directly to the Master's own death. In this final sign, the fourth Gospel plumbs the deepest meaning and significance of Christ for us, the Son of God who is "the resurrection and the life" for those who believe.

The passage from Ezekiel recalls events from salvation history that provide a backdrop to the gospel message. The people of God living in exile are promised by the prophet that the Lord will bring them out of their "graves" (Ezekiel 37:12), reestablishing them in the Promised Land. This is accomplished through the Spirit that will be given to the people, similar to God's original act of creation when the Spirit of the Lord was breathed over the waters, turning chaos into ordered life. The second reading further amplifies the gospel message, employing the image of the Spirit of God who dwells within us and who provides life. Without this Spirit we are mere flesh, a lifeless body. Conversely, that which is mortal is brought

to true life by the same Spirit who "raised Christ from the dead (Romans 3:11)." From the prophet Ezekiel to the apostle Paul, we are brought, step by step, closer to the powerful events of Bethany and the sign of Jesus who brings us out of our graves and plants the Spirit within us.

In the time of Jesus, the rabbis taught that a remnant of life-force or spirit might yet remain near the body of a deceased person for three days. Lazarus' body laid in the tomb for four days and thus was understood to be truly dead. In other raisings that Jesus performed, the deceased had only recently died. In this gospel narrative the evangelist carefully points out (both by Jesus' delayed response in going to Bethany and later when Martha points out that it has been four days since the burial) that the Lazarus called forth from the tomb by Jesus is truly dead. Thus what is revealed is unmistakenly a miracle—worthy of belief.

In Martha's dialogue with Jesus, she professes belief in him as the Lord (*kyrios*), the Messiah and Son of God, the One who is coming into the world. Her belief in Jesus precedes this miracle, while many who witness it "believe in him." In the narrative, Thomas speaks words intended for all believers "Let us go along, to die with him"— or follow Jesus in baptism. The raising of Lazarus from the tomb functions as a template for all believers. Those who die with Christ in baptism also rise to newness of life—are called from the grave of sin and death to new life in Christ.

IMAGES OF PURIFICATION AND ENLIGHTENMENT

Life and Death

In Scripture, from creation onward, life appears as a precious gift which reveals something of God's own mystery and power. God is shown to be full of inexhaustible vitality. God is called "the living God," and highly favors that name (Jeremiah 10:10, NAB). Human life, drawn from the very breath of God (Genesis 2:7), is sacred and depends upon God for its existence.

Death, on the other hand, is a calamity which entered the world because of sin (Romans 5:12, 17; 1 Corinthians 15:21) and is only overcome by Christ's redemptive death and resurrection.

Troubled

When Jesus approaches the tomb, twice the evangelist reports that Jesus is "troubled in spirit" (11:33 and 38). The Greek term *embrimasthai,* which is used, conveys a deep sense of anger, of being stirred up at the deepest level of one's being. At the burial place of Lazarus in Bethany, Jesus angrily confronts the tomb, our graves.

Great emotion highlights the primal or elemental confrontation which takes place in this episode. Even those who believe in Jesus as Lord and Savior will go into the tomb. Physical death is inescapable. Presumably, even Lazarus who was raised from the dead died yet again. In other words, death is not taken away but is overcome and transcended. It is no longer to be feared, for the voice of Jesus will "unlock the gates of life for those who believe." (*Order of Christian Funerals,* "Prayers for Mourners.")

Fidelity

On one level, the second reading and the gospel passage emphasize the response of the believer in faith. But on another level, all of the Scripture readings for this Scrutiny Sunday place at center-stage God's fidelity to us. God will bring us up out of our graves (Ezek 37:12). God who raised Jesus from the dead will raise our mortal bodies from lifelessness (Romans 8:11). As Jesus stands before the tomb of Lazarus, he prays to God, thankful for having been heard so that in this sign "God's glory" (11:4) will be revealed. The psalm text exults in God who is faithful to the covenant and proclaims that mercy and redemption await those who trust in the Lord and await heaven's kindness.

Freedom

When Lazarus emerges from the tomb, he is bound hand and foot in the linen burial cloths, and his face is likewise covered. Jesus commands that he be untied, saying, "let him go free." Freedom is a gift of our redemption (Galations 5:1), and the fruit of our encounter with Jesus, who is the Truth (John 14:5; 8:32, 36).

In Jesus we are freed from that which binds us up and holds us in the tombs of sin, despair, and death. In the Lord whose voice we heed we are let go of the evil that seeks to enslave us and prevent us from living the authentic life of the Spirit.

Love

Unlike the other Scrutiny gospel texts, the main characters of this gospel narrative are all named. They are not anonymous figures but flesh and blood friends of Jesus whom he knew and valued. The evangelist opens this scene with the powerful words, "Jesus loved Martha and her sister and Lazarus" (11:5). We are meant to hear in this how God knows and values each of us and works the miracle of belonging to new life in Jesus.

> *The all-powerful God in loving kindness calls us back to life in company with Christ, whose victory is our redemption. For faithful believers, death is not to be feared, for when our bodies lie in death we gain an everlasting inheritance. For those who follow Jesus, life is changed, not ended. That change begins in baptism when we die to our old selves and rise with Christ to newness of life as temples of the Spirit.*

> *In this season, we celebrate the gifts of life and freedom given in Jesus, whose voice calls us out of the tombs and speaks to us the Word of love.*

(Ordinarily this session will take thirty minutes.)

Getting Started

Gather in the space that has been prepared ahead of time. Include a large basket placed on the floor near the table. Invite everyone to stand and sing (or listen to) "On Eagle's Wings" (Michael Joncas, New Dawn Music, 1979).

Initial Reflection

1. After the participants are seated, lead them in a reflection on the Liturgy of the Word and the Rite of Scrutiny that has just been celebrated:

   Let's take a few minutes to savor the experience of the liturgy that we have just celebrated. Take a deep breath, close your eyes. Think back to arriving at the church this morning. What were you thinking? What were you feeling? (Pause. Hum or sing part or all of the gathering hymn.)
   Father (name) *welcomed us and invited us to prayer. We heard the Word of God proclaimed: "Thus says the Lord . . ." "I will put my spirit in you . . ." "I have promised and I will do it" . . . "the Spirit of God . . . the Spirit of Christ . . . the Spirit dwells in you" . . . "Our beloved Lazarus is dead. . . . Lord, if you had been here. . . . I am the resurrection and the life. . . .Unbind him. . . ." Recall what we heard and saw. Bow your heads and pray. . . . For the* (include here some of the intercessions from the Scrutiny). *. . . God of the living . . . so they may bear witness . . . New life . . . laying on of hands . . . Free them . . . Deliver them . . . Fill them . . . Go forth . . .*

   After several minutes of silence, invite everyone to open their eyes and to share a word or phrase that describes what they experienced. Pause for a moment of silence after each person speaks.

2. Ask the participants to share what their experience of this liturgy and Scrutiny proclaimed about God, about Jesus, about life, about resurrection, and about the importance of a community of faith gathering in prayer to ask for God's deliverance.

3. Invite them to share their experience. Listen attentively so that you can reflect back to the group some of their key words and phrases.

Prayer

Pray or sing the responsorial psalm using "With the Lord There is Mercy" (Michael Joncas, New Dawn Music, GIA Publications, Inc., 1983) or another appropriate song.

(Ordinarily this session will take sixty to ninety minutes.)

Processing

1. Welcome the godparents, sponsors, and other team members. Invite everyone to be seated. Perform or play a recording of a dramatization of today's gospel story, for example, the one found in *Who Calls You By Name*, Vol. II, David Haas, GIA Publications, Inc.

2. Encourage everyone to find a quiet place to reflect alone on today's gospel reading and to pray. Invite them to use one or more of these questions to guide their reflection:

    • Lazarus is in the tomb and wrapped in cloth. In what ways are you entombed, cut off from life, not ready to rise up and to live in a new way? What keeps you from coming out from the tomb when Jesus calls your name?

    • Imagine yourself in the tomb. Jesus is outside, saying powerfully, "(Your name) Come out! Untie him(her). Let him(her) go free. Do you want to come out? Do you want to be free?" What would this mean to you?

    • Jesus is the resurrection and the life, not just for some people, but for each one of us personally. How do you sense Jesus as the resurrection and the life for you now (not just in the next life)?

3. After twenty minutes or so of prayer and reflection, ask the elect and candidates to pair off with their respective godparent or sponsor and share the fruit of their time of prayer and reflection.

4. Allow at least another ten to fifteen minutes for their sharing. Then call everyone back together into the large group.

5. Invite volunteers to share an insight or affirmation they gained from either the individual time of prayer and reflection or from the sharing.

Putting Faith into Practice

1. Encourage everyone to reflect on their election (God's choice of them) and to ponder how much God does love them and calls them by name to be free from all sin—to be unbound, to be truly alive.

2. Encourage them to spend a few minutes each day reflecting on how they are living as people who are given freedom by God or how they are still bound to death, that is, how they are holding themselves back, and perhaps holding others back from living as a people freed from death.

Prayer

Give everyone a piece of paper and ask them to write down what it is that keeps them in death. As they are writing, ask them to ask God to give them life, to unbind them, and to help them go free. When they have finished writing, ask them to put their papers in the basket that is on the floor near the table. Then invite everyone to stand and join in singing or listening to "Jerusalem, My Destiny" (Rory Cooney, GIA Publications, Inc., 1990).

Fifth Sunday of Lent
Year B

The Rich Harvest of the Grain of Wheat

Jeremiah 31:31–34
Psalm 51:3–4, 12–13, 14–15
Hebrews 5:7–9
John 12:20–33

There may be some years in the life of a parish when there are no elect, and the Period of Purification and Enlightenment is celebrated exclusively with baptized candidates preparing for Confirmation and Eucharist and/or Reception into the full communion of the Catholic Church. During these years, the readings used for the Third, Fourth and Fifth Sunday of Lent do not revert to Year A, since the Scrutinies are not celebrated for the baptized candidates. However, because the period being celebrated is nevertheless one of purification and enlightenment, this background on the Scripture readings and their images is offered.

Greeks were in Jerusalem for the Passover festival, participating in the Temple worship. That these Gentiles were active in observing the Passover means that they were Gentiles sympathetic to Judaism and possibly even proselytes, meaning "Godfearers." Moreover, they wished to see Jesus.

Recall the beginning of the Fourth Gospel when the disciples of John the Baptist are intrigued by Jesus and they ask him where he is staying, and Jesus responds, "come and see" (1:46, NAB). Again, the man born blind who is healed and who comes to believe in Jesus is prompted with the words, "you have seen him!" (9:37, NAB).

The ability to see, in John's Gospel, functions more than on the biological level. "To see" symbolizes insight, belief, and acceptance of "the Light of the world" who is Jesus. These gentile sympathizers seek out Jesus whom they wish "to see." This marvelous wonder, that even gentiles are seeking him out, is the occasion for Jesus to proclaim that it is now his "hour." This is not a measure of time as in chronological moments, any more than sight in John's Gospel is mere physical seeing. The "hour" of Jesus is the special, graced moment when the ages of the world are transfixed by his suffering, death, and resurrection. *Hour* in Greek is not *chronos* but *kairos*, God's time.

As the Fourth Gospel builds to the arrest and passion of Jesus when he is "lifted up" in Jerusalem, *kairos* is invoked and a voice, like thunder, is heard from heaven. Similar to the accounts of Jesus' baptism and his Transfiguration, the voice speaks of glorification. Now, in this moment, in this special time, God's name is glorified in Jesus who will draw all—Jews, Greeks, everyone—to himself.

IMAGES OF PURIFICATION AND ENLIGHTENMENT

The Grain of Wheat

Jesus is arrested as a rabble-rouser. He is sentenced as a common criminal. He dies an awful death. He is entombed hurriedly before the Passover commences. The suffering and death of the man from Nazareth seems, on the surface, so inconsequential, so meaningless. But like the grain of wheat, small and insignificant, that goes into the ground and dies, his death produces great fruit, a stalk of wheat that blossoms into food for the life of the world, bread that is broken in the Eucharist and becomes the mystery of which believers partake—the sacrament that makes the Church.

The man from Nazareth, who learned a carpenter's trade at the knee of his foster father, has built a great household of worship. Christ is the source of eternal salvation for those who believe.

Obedience

The gospel passage for this Sunday reports that Jesus' "soul is troubled now" and that his hour has come (12:27). Jesus is truly the Son of God become human. In this passage, Jesus exhibits feelings. Elsewhere in the Fourth Gospel he weeps at the tomb of Lazarus and over Jerusalem and sweats blood.

This passage in the Fourth Gospel functions as the Johannine Gethsemane. Jesus seems not to relish the prospect of the cross and death, and yet he goes forward in obedience to the will of the Father, for this hour is the hour of glory—the glory of the Father.

Paul's letter to the Hebrews speaks of Christ's obedience which *perfected* him (5:9). This is a special term which indicates the conferral of priestly status. Christ does what priests do: offers "prayers and supplications" (11:7), and offers himself as a willing sacrifice.

The Law Written Upon Hearts

The Law given to Moses on Sinai was etched upon stone tablets. The prophet Jeremiah expresses that the day will come when this written law will be internalized upon believing hearts. Christians see in this the stance of believers who embrace the One who is the way, the truth, and the life.

Hearts that are open to Christ are filled with the power of his love and are given, as today's psalm states, a "steadfastness," and a "renewed spirit." Clean hearts are the gift of those who open themselves to see Jesus and what he has to offer.

The God who established his covenant with the people so long ago will write the law of love upon hearts that are open to grace. That love is lifted high in Christ who gave his life for us on the cross. Wounded for our sakes, blood and water flowed from his side, the fountain of sacramental life in the Church.

In this season, we celebrate the Savior's heart, open, inviting all to draw water in joy from the springs of salvation.

(Ordinarily this session will take thirty minutes.)

This session is used when there are no elect but only baptized candidates preparing to complete their Christian initiation or to be received into the full communion of the Catholic Church.

Getting Started

Gather in the space that has been prepared ahead of time. Include sheaves of wheat, grains of wheat, and a flower pot in the space. Invite everyone to be seated. Light the candle. Give each person a grain of wheat to hold as you play or sing "Unless a Grain of Wheat" (Bernadette Farrell, OCP Publications, 1983).

Initial Reflection

1. Ask the candidates to close their eyes. Lead them in a reflection, such as:

    Take a few deep breaths. Feel the grain of wheat in your hand. (Pause.)

    Rub it around in your hand as you think about the potential contained in this single grain of wheat: thirty or fifty or one hundred fold if it is buried in the earth, given water and sunlight. However, if you keep the grain in your hand, it will remain but a grain.

2. Proclaim John 12:23–24 from today's gospel reading.

3. After several minutes, invite the candidates to open their eyes. Invite them to share what they were thinking, feeling, sensing, or hearing during the reflection. Gather the responses from them.

4. Ask what this reflection has to do with the Liturgy of the Word celebrated today. Connect the liturgy and the gospel parable of the grain of wheat to the whole season of Lent, explaining that Lent is a time to step back and look at our lives to determine what is of God and what is of sin. Also, remind them that there are only two more weeks before the Easter season begins.

5. Ask them to share in a few words what the message of today's gospel reading is.

Prayer

(Have quiet music ready to be played in the background.) Give each candidate a piece of paper shaped like a seed and ask them to write on it ways they can die to selfishness and sin. After a few minutes, ask them to wad up their paper seed and bring it forth and put it in the flower pot, asking God to help them to die to sin. After everyone has done so, allow for a few moments of quiet reflection before the break.

(Ordinarily this session will take sixty to ninety minutes.)

Processing

1. Welcome the sponsors and other team members. Sing or play again "Unless a Grain of Wheat" by Bernadette Farrell. Invite everyone to be seated.

2. Proclaim John 12:20–33, today's gospel message.

3. Give each person a copy of Handout 14, which has these questions for reflection. Ask them to consider using one or more of them:

   • The Greeks wanted to see Jesus. In what ways have I been able to see Jesus? In what ways do I bring others to see Jesus?

   • Jesus says that those who want to serve him will follow him. When do I find it easy to follow Jesus? When do I find it difficult to follow Jesus?

   • Jesus says that those who love their life in this world will lose it and those who hate their life in this world will gain eternal life. In what ways am I attempting to make this world heaven, and losing sight of eternal life?

4. After fifteen to twenty minutes of quiet reflection, ask candidates to discuss their reflection with their sponsors.

5. After an additional ten to fifteen minutes, gather everyone back together and invite them to share the insights, affirmations, and challenges they gained from their reflection and discussion.

Putting Faith into Practice

1. Encourage candidates and their sponsors to get together during this week to review the sacrament of Reconciliation. If the parish is going to celebrate a communal celebration of Penance, encourage the candidates and sponsors to participate in it.

2. Suggest that everyone review how they are fulfilling their chosen Lenten practices and renewing their efforts to be faithful to them.

Prayer

Invite the participants to think about one thing God is asking them to change, and to formulate a petition asking for God's help to make this change. Invite those who wish to pray their petition aloud to do so. When all have finished praying their petitions, conclude the prayer in these or similar words:

> *God, you have planted within us the seeds of mercy and love. Nurture these longings that the fruit which these seeds bring forth might be a source of new life for our world. We ask this in the name of Jesus Christ, our brother. Amen.*

Sing "Jerusalem, My Destiny" (Rory Cooney, GIA Publications, Inc., 1990).

Fifth Sunday of Lent
Year C

The Woman Caught in Adultery

Isaiah 43:16–21
Psalm 126:1–6
Philippians 3:8–14
John 8:1–11

There may be some years in the life of a parish when there are no elect, and the period of purification and enlightenment is celebrated exclusively with baptized candidates for Confirmation and Eucharist, and/or Reception into the full communion of the Catholic Church. During those years, the readings used for the Third, Fourth and Fifth Sunday of Lent do not revert to Year A, since the Scrutinies are not celebrated for the baptized candidates. However, because the period being celebrated is nevertheless one of purification and enlightenment, this background on the Scripture readings and their images is offered.

In the first reading, this portion of the Book of the Prophet Isaiah deals with Israel's return from exile in Babylon. Those who had been deported saw in their return to the Promised Land a New Exodus. The initial rescue of Israel out of slavery in Egypt became the primal faith experience upon which all other subsequent deliverance was imagined. The prophet announces for the Lord, "remember not the events of the past, the things of long ago consider not" (43:18) as a way of saying that the relationship solidified long ago in the exodus experience was being lived anew in the action of God. Thus, the Most High exclaims, "See, I am doing something new! Now it springs forth . . ." (43:19). The past is not a dead thing, unrelated to the present. The covenant relationship between God and God's people continues even today as

the events of the present, understood in the light of the past, bring to birth the future.

The poignant scene of the woman caught in adultery does not appear in the earliest manuscripts of John's Gospel. Various explanations by scholars are given for this omission, including the possibility of the early Christians' discomfort at the ease with which Jesus accepts the woman who is caught in sin—as compared with their own rigorous penitential practice for serious sinners. Whether this explanation accounts for the omission or not, this scene does appear in the Vulgate, Saint Jerome's version, and the authenticity of this passage is not questioned.

There is no doubt that the woman sinned. Yet the focus of the passage is not so much on the sinner caught in sin or even on the forgiveness granted by Jesus, but rather on the self-righteous attitude of those who confront Jesus and attempt to trap him by this example. The consequence of being caught in adultery would be death, even though the Romans reserved capital punishment to themselves. Whether she would actually be stoned or not, Jesus is in an awkward position, for he must side with either the Mosaic Law or the Roman occupiers. Perhaps the scribes and Pharisees depicted in the passage resent the crowds that are attracted to Jesus' teaching and wish to recapture attention to their own teaching role. In any case, they have the necessary witnesses, she was caught in the act, and she has now been brought before Jesus and the crowds. They "made her stand there in front of everyone" (8:3).

This public exposure is the position for an official legal questioning and investigation (Daniel 8 exhibits parallels, although in the Old Testament scene, Susanna is innocent). When the scribes and Pharisees ask Jesus' opinion in the case, he merely bends down and "started tracing on the ground with his finger" (8:6). Perhaps by this action Jesus cleverly mimics the Roman legal practice of the judge who first writes out the accusation as legal proceedings begin. While there is no way to ascertain what or why Jesus wrote, his writing portrays him as one who is in control, who responds in his own good time to the trap which is laid for him. It is his statement about the one without sin that stops the accusers cold and leaves him alone with the woman to offer her a chance at new life, leaving behind the way of sin.

IMAGES OF PURIFICATION AND ENLIGHTENMENT

"Neither Do I Condemn You" (John 8:11, NAB)

Elsewhere in the Gospel of John, Jesus exclaims, "I did not come to condemn the world but to save the world" (12:47). Jesus' statement at the end of the encounter with the woman caught in adultery conforms to the theme in the Fourth Gospel that condemnation is not part of the mission of Christ. Those who are condemned, in effect, have passed judgment on themselves by their blindness, by not embracing the way of life shown by Jesus.

Return and Restoration

Both the first reading and the psalm text for today's liturgy emphasize the greatness of God who not only rescues but who restores Israel to the promised land. Indeed, "[t]he Lord had done great things for us; Oh, how happy we were!" (126:3)

Racing to Grasp the Prize

In his letter to the Philippians Paul uses the image of the believer who runs in the race, eyes fixed on the finish line. Racing to grasp the prize, the believer has already been grasped by Christ in baptism. One is not quite there, and yet it is within reach. By the gift of Jesus' sacrifice, forgiveness is granted, a chance for new life is freely given, and all else is but "rubbish" (3:8). The Lord alone is the wealth put into the hands of believers.

God restores Israel to the Promised Land and the future unfolds according to divine providence. The Lord does great things for us. Rejoice!

Self-righteousness has no place before Jesus, the Christ, who can judge the heart. In this season, we celebrate our freedom from sin and the lease on new life we have been given by the sacrifice of Jesus.

(Ordinarily this session will take thirty minutes.)

> *This session is used when there are no elect, only candidates to complete their Christian initiation or to be received into the full communion of the Catholic Church.*

Getting Started

Gather in the space that has been prepared ahead of time. Include a cross on the center table. Invite everyone to be seated. Light the candle. Play instrumental music softly as you take the cross to each candidate. Invite each candidate to hold it for a few moments before you take it and give it to the next candidate. After all have had an opportunity to hold the cross, place it back on the table. Allow for a few more minutes of silent prayer.

Initial Reflection

1. Invite everyone to close their eyes and reflect on the Liturgy of the Word which has just been celebrated. Then if anyone wishes, invite them to share a word or phrase they heard or name a feeling they experienced during the celebration.

2. Have everyone close their eyes and listen as you slowly and deliberately proclaim John 8:1–11. (Pause.) Repeat verse 7 in which Jesus says let anyone who is without sin cast the first stone. (Pause.) Repeat the dialogue between Jesus and the woman found in verses 10 and 11 in which Jesus says that he does not condemn the woman but tells her to commit that sin no more. (Pause.)

3. Invite the candidates to reflect on these elements of the story:

   - Jesus does not condemn the woman but offers her forgiveness and a new life.

   - Jesus condemns the self-righteous attitude of those scribes and Pharisees who would not forgive the woman.

4. Ask them to ponder: What sin could you be brought forward and accused of before God? Then have them imagine the dialogue they would have with Jesus following such an accusation.

5. Emphasize with the candidates that Jesus offers us deliverance from our sin. Jesus offers us new life—however, we must be willing to change.

Prayer

Use these words from Eucharistic Prayer for Masses of Reconciliation II, Roman Missal.

> *God of power and might,*
> *we praise you through your Son, Jesus Christ,*
> *who comes in your name.*
> *He is the word that brings salvation.*
> *He is the hand you stretch out to sinners.*
> *He is the way that leads to your peace.*
> *God our Father,*
> *we had wandered far from you,*
> *but through your Son you have brought us*
>   *back.*
> *You gave him up to death*
> *so that we might turn again to you*
> *and find our way to one another.*
> *Therefore we celebrate the reconciliation*
> *Christ has gained for us.*

(Ordinarily this session will take sixty to ninety minutes.)

Processing

1. Welcome the sponsors and other team members. After everyone is seated proclaim the second reading: Paul's letter to the Philippians 3:8–14.

2. After a few moments of silence, give everyone a copy of a Handout 15 which has the following questions to guide their reflections:

   • Think back to the beginning of your initiation journey. Who or what prompted you to approach this parish community to inquire about the Catholic faith?

   • In what ways is your faith journey similar to the race that Paul describes in his letter to the Philippians?

   • What training do you need in order to continue the race?

   • Think about the finish line—which is not the end of this initiation process but, rather, heaven. What do you need to do to keep on the track and be faithful to the race?

3. After fifteen to twenty minutes of silent reflection, invite sponsors and candidates to get together and share their reflections.

4. After ten to fifteen minutes, invite everyone to gather back together. Ask them to share the insights, affirmations, and challenges the gained from their reflection and sharing.

Putting Faith into Practice

1. Invite everyone to continue during the week to reflect on their initiation journey and how God has led them to this time and place.

2. Encourage them to name who and what distracts them from the race and who or what supports and encourages them to keep in the race.

Prayer

Invite sponsors to stand behind their candidates and place their hands on their candidate's shoulders as you pray:

> *God, Creator of all life,*
> *you have gifted us with these wonderful*
>   *candidates who seek to find you.*
> *Bless them in a special way this week.*
> *Strengthen them in their resolve to run the*
>   *race and to seek you in all things.*
> *Guide them as they find their way to you.*
> *You are the one they seek.*
> *We ask this in Jesus' name. Amen.*

Passion (Palm) Sunday
Year A, B, and C

The Procession with Palms
and
The Passion of Our Lord

The Procession with Palms:
Year A   Matthew 21:1–11
Year B   Mark 11:1–10 or John 12:12–16
Year C   Luke 19:28–40

Liturgy of the Word (Year A, B, C):
Isaiah 50:4–7
Psalm 22:8–9, 17–18, 19–20, 23–24
Philippians 2:6–11
Passion narrative references, see below

Each year, on this Sunday, the liturgy recalls the events surrounding the triumphal entry of Jesus into Jerusalem and his subsequent arrest, trial, crucifixion, death, and entombment. Within this one Sunday celebration an immense and varied body of Scripture is proclaimed. Not only the emotional tone of these readings differ, but the images presented are contrasting. First, the Church proclaims gospel texts which depict the acclamation of the crowds as Jesus entered the Temple city. In Year A, as Jesus enters, we hear that "all this has come to pass that the writings of the prophets may be fulfilled" (26:56) typical of Matthew's Gospel, which is so intent on showing Jesus as the fulfillment of the Old Covenant. In Year B, as Jesus enters, the crowd cries out "Hosanna!" (11:9), which translates, "Save us!" This is typical of Mark's terse, to-the-point style. In Year C, as Jesus enters, the crowd of disciples echoes

the angels' exultation of birth at the beginning of Luke's Gospel, "Glory to God in the highest on earth peace to those on whom his favor rests" (1:14). Next, in the first reading for Mass, we meditate on the image of the Suffering Servant from the prophet Isaiah. This passage is amplified by the powerful Psalm 22. The second reading offers to us the sublime Pauline hymn which extols Jesus Christ who "emptied himself, taking the form of a slave" (2:7), only to be raised up to glory.

Image after overwhelming image is laid before us. But, as if this is not enough Scripture to be immersed into one celebration of the liturgy, the Church then solemnly proclaims the Passion narrative. All the readings draw us in and swamp our imaginations, carrying us beyond ourselves so that we truly do what we are meant to do in the liturgy; that is, not hold back, but in remembering and retelling, recall the event as a living reality. The Word—who even now continues to enter into our lives, saving us, opening us to the peace of heaven, and establishing among us the New Covenant in his blood—is made present in these many proclamations.

To deepen our understanding the Liturgy of the Word proclaimed on Passion Sunday, details from each gospel account of the Passion narrative will be presented. These highlights are selected to illustrate the unique characteristics of each synoptic account.

Year A: Passion
Matthew 26:14–27, 66

Matthew's Gospel contains many allusions to the Hebrew Scriptures, presenting Jesus as the fulfillment of the Law and the embodiment of the New Covenant (see Matthew 5:17). When violence erupts in support of freeing Jesus, he commands his supporters to desist, citing the fulfillment of Scriptures (26:54). In the Passion narrative, there are four allusions to the Hebrew Scriptures: Matthew 26:16 (which echoes Zechariah 11:12); Matthew 26:26 (which echoes Exodus 24:8); Matthew 27:29 (which echoes Isaiah 50:4–7, the first reading); and Matthew 27:46 (which echoes Psalm 22, the psalm text for today's liturgy).

Only in Matthew 27:62–66 do we read the details about the guard being stationed at Jesus' tomb as a result of a prophetic utterance by the Lord. In response to the leaders' request Pilate orders the tomb to be secured. No human agency will be able to secure or suppress either the Old Testament prophecy or the new prophecy found in the Jesus event.

Year B: Passion
Mark 14:1–15:47

As Jesus is arrested in Mark's account, a young man (*neaniskos*) flees naked, leaving behind his cloth (*sindon*). When the women come to the tomb to provide proper burial, that is, anointing of Jesus' body, they discover a "young man" (16:5)—not an "angel"—sitting on the right side, the place of honor.

Could this young man be symbolic of the catechumens in the Marcan community? A young man runs away naked at the arrest of Jesus because he is afraid to be associated with this martyrdom. Only when one professes faith, witnessing to the Son of God (15:39), and only when one is not afraid to die with Jesus in the womb or tomb of baptism, will one be clothed in the white garment (16:5) of the neophyte, who proclaims the Resurrection and the triumph over evil.

This victory over sin and evil is manifested in Jesus' loud cry on the cross (15:34, 37). When Jesus heals, evil cries out (see Mark 1:26; 5:7).

Year C: Passion
Luke 22:14–23:56

Only in the Gospel according to Luke does the Passion narrative open with the leadership plotting against Jesus because they were "afraid of the people" (22:2) and have the Master himself say, "I have eagerly desired to eat this Passover with you" (22:15). These events which depict a New Passover inaugurating the dominion of God have been "determined" (22:22) according to the plan of heaven.

In spite of this plan, which unfolds and is accomplished in Jesus, the Master of these events nevertheless experiences things intensely, sweating drops of blood as he prays (22:44) in anguish. Yet, in the midst of his passion and this pain, Luke alone reports that Jesus makes the effort to continue his ministry, healing the ear of the high priest's slave (22:51).

Jesus, who is innocent (23:4, 14, 22, 47) and unjustly condemned, forgives from the cross (23:34). The divine plan of mercy unfolds in Jesus' passion.

(Ordinarily this session will take thirty minutes.)

IMAGES OF PURIFICATION AND ENLIGHTENMENT

Passover Meal

All the synoptic Gospels present the last supper of Jesus with his disciples in a similar fashion. He eats and drinks the passover meal with them, breaking bread and offering a common cup, identifying himself with the bread and wine. He uses the term "new covenant," deliberately recalling the original covenant God made with Moses on Sinai. The promise of the New Covenant is sealed by his own blood.

The images of the passover meal and the blood of the covenant are steeped in the Hebrew Scriptures. By the ministry and mission of Jesus, especially by his suffering, death, and resurrection, these ancient images are given a unique meaning for all time. Those who followed Jesus and witnessed to his Resurrection, from the first days of the Church down to our own time, remember his saving sacrifice in the meal of the Eucharist: the body and blood of Christ made present for us once again by the grace of God.

Betrayal, Denial, and Desertion

According to the various synoptic accounts, Judas betrays Jesus, Peter denies any association or knowledge of the Master, and the remaining disciples flee at his arrest. Of all these narrative pieces, the synoptics and John are most in agreement in reporting that Peter, who earlier acclaimed Jesus as Messiah, emphatically denies Jesus, and after doing so breaks down and weeps bitterly. This is at the very moment that Jesus stands before the council and proclaims clearly who he is (Matthew 26:64, Mark 14:62, and Luke 22:70).

After the arrest of Jesus, when all flee, Peter follows behind hesitantly. Lurking in the shadows, he is spied by the firelight. When challenged, he fears for his own life and denies any involvement with Jesus. Not only does this gospel episode capture the imagination of the hearer but it also gives every follower of Jesus hope—for we are all human, and if in some measure we do not betray and desert the Master, we do, at times, deny him.

(Ordinarily this session will take sixty to ninety minutes.)

Crucifixion, Breathing His Last, and the Curtain Torn in Two

The climax of the Passion narratives is Jesus being nailed to a cross, dying a hideous death. And as Jesus breathes his last breath, the three synoptic Gospels report that the Temple curtain is torn in two, from top to bottom and down the middle (Matthew 27:51, Mark 15:38, Luke 23:45). The tearing, or rending, of the curtain echoes the earlier action of the high priest as he tears his robes upon hearing Jesus' blasphemy and demands his death. Early Christians saw in the torn curtain God's response (anger) at the unjust death of Jesus.

Whether the early Christians were correct in their reading, the symbol of the torn curtain certainly recalls the earlier gospel episode when the heavens are torn, or rent, at Jesus' baptism and his ministry is inaugurated (see Mark 1:10). This moment, at his death, is also an inauguration—this time the inauguration of the dominion of God, in which, because of the sacrifice of Jesus, there is no curtain now separating people from the Holy of Holies. Authentic worship now takes place in Jesus and his dying breath is like the breath of God, creating something new, the Church.

Entombment

After his death, Jesus is entombed. By his own burial, Jesus makes holy the graves of all who die believing. Even though the tomb claims our mortal bodies, we rise with Christ to newness of life beyond the grave by the gift of new life in baptism. The final resting place of believers is not meant to be their earthly tomb but the arms of God who, as the psalmist asserts will be praised "in the midst of the assembly" (Psalm 22:23). For the Lord alone is our deliverance from the grave of sin and death.

Paschal Mystery

Taken together, we name the suffering, death, entombment, resurrection, ascension, and bestowing the Spirit upon the Church the Paschal Mystery of Jesus Christ. As we enter into Holy Week, the liturgy begins to unfold for us the Paschal mystery—the gospel message that will be proclaimed and celebrated fully during the Easter Triduum.

> *The God of our ancestors has not abandoned us, but by his mercy and love has raised up for us a Savior, Jesus Christ. The New Covenant is established by his blood, a Church is born by his dying breath and eternal life is guaranteed by his cross.*

> *In this season of purification and enlightenment, we who follow the Master pass over with him and embrace all the good things that the dominion of God promises us.*

(Ordinarily this session will take thirty minutes.)

Getting Started

Gather in the space that has been prepared ahead of time. Have a red cloth placed over the purple one, and include on the table palm branches and a cross. Gather the elect and candidates and ask them to stand in a circle. Make sure each participant is holding a palm branch. Proclaim Matthew 21:1–11 the Gospel for "The Procession with Palms," Year A. Then invite everyone to be seated.

Initial Reflection

1. Invite the elect and candidates to share words, phrases, sights, sounds, and feelings they heard or experienced in today's liturgy.

2. Lead the participants in a reflection on the different parts of today's liturgy using these or similar directions:

    Close your eyes and recall the first part of our liturgy. As we arrived we were given palm branches to carry and asked to assemble in a different place (perhaps outside). The priest wearing red greeted us with the words, Today, we begin this solemn celebration in union with the whole Church. We heard the Gospel proclaim that as Jesus rode into Jerusalem, a great throng of people greeted him. (Pause.) In the Liturgy of the Word, we heard Isaiah describe the Suffering Servant who gave his back to those who would beat him and called upon the Lord God to help him. Paul directed us to have the attitude of Christ . . . as Christ emptied himself . . . took the form of a slave . . . obediently accepting even death, death on a cross. The Passion was proclaimed (Pause.) We listened to the homily (include words and phrases). We were sent forth until that day—soon—when you will join us at the eucharistic table. (Pause.)

3. Invite everyone to reflect on the celebration of today's liturgy. Then invite responses to these questions: What did this liturgy proclaim about Christ? About his death and resurrection? What did this liturgy proclaim about Christ's followers?

4. After a few responses lead everyone in prayer.

Prayer

Invite everyone to stand again, holding their palm branches. Lead them in praying a litany of praise. After each invocation, ask them to respond by chanting (or saying) the refrain "Hosanna to the Son of David."

> *Jesus, healer of the blind, the lame and the sick,* (refrain)
> *Jesus, teacher and preacher to the crowds,* (refrain)
> *Jesus, maker of miracles,* (refrain)
> *Jesus, who brings the dead to life,* (refrain)
> *Jesus, son of Mary and Joseph,* (refrain)
> *Jesus, challenger of the self-righteous,* (refrain)
> *Jesus, champion of the poor, the widowed and the orphaned,* (refrain)

Conclude by singing "All Glory, Laud, and Honor" (attributed to Saint Theodulph), which can be found in most worship aids.

(Ordinarily this session will take sixty to ninety minutes.)

Processing

1. Welcome godparents, sponsors, and other team members and ask them to sit with their respective elect or candidate.

2. Recall with everyone key images and events from the Passion narrative proclaimed in today's liturgy by repeating phrases and naming characters and their roles. Also include the names of key places and actions such as the upper room, the washing of feet, the Mount of Olives, Gethsemane, the gathering place of the Sanhedrin, the courtyard, Golgotha, and so on.

3. Invite each pair of participants to discuss: What is becoming clearer to you about having a relationship with Jesus Christ and what does such a relationship involve?

4. After eight to ten minutes of discussion, ask them to share insights and affirmations they gained about what it means to be claimed by Christ in Baptism.

5. Next, invite the pairs to discuss these questions:

   - In what ways do you feel or think you have already begun to embrace discipleship?

   - What do you feel or think will be the greatest challenge as you grow and deepen your relationship with Jesus Christ?

6. After ten to fifteen minutes of discussion, ask everyone to come back together in the large group. Ask volunteers to share the challenges they think they will face.

Putting Faith into Practice

1. Review with everyone that Lent ends with sundown on Holy Thursday and that the Easter Triduum begins with the celebration of "The Evening Mass of the Lord's Supper" on Holy Thursday. Be sure to announce the times for the Triduum services.

2. Speak briefly about Good Friday and Holy Saturday. (See pages 107–110 and 136–137 of this manual.)

3. Encourage them to spend time in prayer and reflection in anticipation of the Easter Vigil.

Prayer

Give everyone a piece of paper. Invite them to recall what someone in the group said would be, or is, the greatest challenge to being a disciple of Jesus Christ. Ask them to write a petition for that person, asking God to strengthen her or him to meet the challenge. After everyone has had time to do this, invite everyone to stand in a circle. Explain that after your opening prayer anyone who wishes may read their petition and after each petition the entire group will sing (or say) *O Lord, Hear our Prayer.* Then begin your prayer:

> *Jesus, you promised that whenever two or three were gathered in your name, you would be in their midst. We count on that promise in a particular way today. Hear our prayers for one another.*

Conclude by praying the Our Father together.

(Ordinarily this session will take thirty minutes.)

Getting Started

Gather in the space that has been prepared ahead of time. Have a red cloth placed over the purple one, and include on the table palm branches and a cross. Gather the elect and candidates and ask them to stand in a circle. Make sure each participant is holding a palm branch. Proclaim Mark 11:1–10, the Gospel for "The Procession with Palms," Year B. Then invite everyone to be seated.

Initial Reflection

1. Invite the elect and candidates to share words, phrases, sights, sounds, and feelings they heard or experienced in today's liturgy.

2. Lead the participants in a reflection on today's liturgy using these or similar directions:

   Close your eyes and recall the first part of our liturgy. As we arrived we were given palm branches to carry and asked to assemble in a different place (perhaps outside). The priest wearing red greeted us with the words, "Today, we begin this solemn celebration in union with the whole Church." We heard the Gospel proclaim that as Jesus rode into Jerusalem, a great throng of people greeted him. (Pause.) *In the Liturgy of the Word, we heard Isaiah describe the Suffering Servant who gave his back to those who beat him and who called upon the Lord God to help him. Paul directed us to have the attitude of Christ . . . as Christ emptied himself . . . took the form of a slave . . . obediently accepting even death, death on a cross. The Passion was proclaimed.* (Pause.) *We listened to this homily* (include words and phrases) (Pause.) *We were sent forth until that day—soon—when you will join us at the eucharistic table.* (Pause.)

3. Invite responses to these questions: What did this Liturgy proclaim about Christ? About his death and resurrection? What did this Liturgy proclaim about Christ's followers?

4. After several responses lead them into prayer.

Prayer

Invite everyone to stand again holding their palm branches. Lead them in praying a litany of praise. After each invocation, ask them to respond by chanting (or saying) the refrain "Hosanna to the Son of David."

> *Jesus, healer of the blind, the lame and the sick,* (refrain)
> *Jesus, teacher and preacher to the crowds,* (refrain)
> *Jesus, maker of miracles,* (refrain)
> *Jesus, who brings the dead to life,* (refrain)
> *Jesus, son of Mary and Joseph,* (refrain)
> *Jesus, challenger of the self-righteous,* (refrain)
> *Jesus, champion of the poor, the widowed and the orphaned,* (refrain)

Conclude by singing "All Glory, Laud, and Honor" (attributed to Saint Theodulph), which can be found in most worship aids.

(Ordinarily this session will take sixty to ninety minutes.)

Processing

1. Welcome godparents, sponsors, and other team members and ask them to sit with their respective elect or candidate.

2. Recall with everyone images and events from the Passion narrative proclaimed in today's liturgy. For example: the Passover Meal, the New Covenant, Judas' betrayal, Peter's denial, desertion of all, the Crucifixion, Jesus breathing his last, the tomb, the Paschal mystery, and so on.

3. Invite everyone to choose one of the images or events that were recalled from the Passion narrative. Ask them to spend some time reflecting on the image or event by asking:

    Where are you? (Pause.) *What are you seeing?* (Pause.) *Hearing?* (Pause.) *Feeling?* (Pause.) *Jesus approaches you and the two of you begin to have a conversation. What would Jesus say to you?* (Pause.) *What would you say to Jesus?* (Pause.)

4. After ten to fifteen minutes of reflection, ask them to open their eyes. Invite the elect to pair with their godparents and candidates with sponsors, to spend about five minutes sharing their conversation with Jesus.

5. Gather the participants back together. Invite a sharing of insights and affirmations gleaned from their discussions.

Putting Faith into Practice

1. Review with everyone that Lent ends with sundown on Holy Thursday and that the Easter Triduum begins with the celebration of "The Evening Mass of the Lord's Supper" on Holy Thursday. Be sure to announce the times for the Triduum services.

2. Speak briefly about Good Friday and Holy Saturday. (See pages 107–110 and 136–137 in this manual.)

3. Encourage them to spend time in prayer and reflection in anticipation of the Easter Vigil.

Prayer

Ask the elect and candidates to be seated and their respective godparents and sponsors to stand behind them. Invite the godparents and sponsors to place their hands on the shoulders of their elect or candidate and pray for them that they be open to God's invitation to enter more deeply into a relationship with God. Conclude by singing "Tree of Life" (Marty Haugen, GIA Publications, Inc., 1984).

(Ordinarily this session will take thirty minutes.)

Getting Started

Gather in the space that has been prepared ahead of time. Have a red cloth placed over the purple one and include on the table palm branches and a cross. Gather the elect and candidates and ask them to stand in a circle. Make sure each participant is holding a palm branch. Proclaim John 12:12–16, the Gospel for "The Procession with Palms," Year C. Then invite everyone to be seated.

Initial Reflection

1. Invite the elect and candidates to share words, phrases, sights, sounds, and feelings they heard or experienced in today's liturgy.

2. Lead the participants in a reflection on today's liturgy, using these or similar words:

   Close your eyes and recall the first part of our liturgy. As we arrived we were given palm branches to carry and asked to assemble in a different place (perhaps outside). The priest wearing red greeted us with the words, "Today we begin this solemn celebration in union with the whole Church." We heard the Gospel proclaim that as Jesus rode into Jerusalem, a great throng of people greeted him. (Pause.) In the Liturgy of the Word, we heard Isaiah describe the Suffering Servant who gave his back to those who beat him and who called upon the Lord God to help him Paul directed us to have the attitude of Christ . . . as Christ emptied himself . . . took the form of a slave . . . obediently accepting even death, death on a cross. The Passion was proclaimed. (Pause.) We listened to the homily (include words and/or phrases).
   We were sent forth until that day—soon— when you will join us at the eucharistic table. (Pause.)

3. Invite responses to these questions: What did this Liturgy proclaim about Christ? About his death and resurrection? What did this Liturgy proclaim about Christ's followers?

4. After several responses lead them into prayer.

Prayer

Invite everyone to stand again holding their palm branches. Lead them in praying a litany of praise. After each invocation, ask them to respond by chanting (or saying) the refrain "Hosanna to the Son of David."

   Jesus, healer of the blind, the lame and the sick, (refrain)
   Jesus, teacher and preacher to the crowds, (refrain)
   Jesus, maker of miracles, (refrain)
   Jesus, who brings the dead to life, (refrain)
   Jesus, son of Mary and Joseph, (refrain)
   Jesus, challenger of the self-righteous, (refrain)
   Jesus, champion of the poor, the widowed, and the orphaned, (refrain) . . .

Conclude by singing "All Glory, Laud, and Honor" (attributed to Saint Theodulph), which can be found in most worship aids.

(Ordinarily this session will take sixty to ninety minutes.)

Processing

1. Welcome godparents, sponsors, and other team members and ask them to sit with their respective elect or candidate. Sing several times "Jesus, Remember Me" (Les Presses de Taize, 1981).

2. Give them handout 18 which contains these questions:

   • Which person in the Passion narrative do you identify with? Why?

   • What is becoming clearer to you about the meaning of discipleship?

   • As you approach the time of your baptism or the renewal of your baptism and reception into the full communion of the Catholic Church, what do you want to pray for?

   Tell them to consider one or more of the questions. Give them fifteen to twenty minutes to reflect alone and then join with godparents and sponsors, and discuss in pairs their questions and reflections.

3. After ten to fifteen minutes of sharing, gather everyone back into the large group. Invite a sharing of the insights, affirmations, and challenges they gained from reflection and discussion.

Putting Faith into Practice

1. Review with everyone that Lent ends with sundown on Holy Thursday and that the Easter Triduum begins with the "Evening Mass of the Lord's Supper" on Holy Thursday. Be sure to announce the times for the Triduum services.

2. Speak briefly about Good Friday and Holy Saturday. (See pages 107–110 and 136–137 of this manual.)

3. Encourage them to spend time in prayer and reflection in anticipation of the Easter Vigil.

Prayer

Ask the elect and candidates to be seated and their respective godparents and sponsors to stand behind them. Sing "Jesus, Remember Me" several times. Invite the godparents and sponsors to place their hands on the shoulders of their elect or candidate and pray for them that they be open to God's invitation to them and that they stand firm in their desire to embrace discipleship. Pray together the Our Father and conclude by singing several times "Jesus, Remember Me."

Holy Thursday
Year A, B, and C

Mass of the Lord's Supper

Exodus 12:1–8, 11–14
Psalm 116:12–13, 15–16, 17–18
1 Corinthians 11:23–26
John 13:1–15

The *General Norms for the Liturgical Year and the Calendar* (Washington D.C.: USCC, 1976) emphasizes the unity of "the Easter triduum of the passion and resurrection of Christ [which is] the culmination of the entire liturgical year" (18). "The Easter triduum begins with the evening Mass of the Lord's Supper, reaches its high point in the Easter Vigil, and closes with evening prayer on Easter Sunday" (19). A sense of the unity of these days is found early on in the Church, as is evident from a letter of Saint Ambrose (d. 397) regarding the celebration of Easter: "We must observe both the days of the passion and resurrection, so that there may be a day of woe and a day of joy, a fast-day and a feast-day . . . This is the holy Triduum . . . during which Christ suffered, was buried and rose again." (Letter 23, in J. P. Migne, *Patrolgia latina*, 16, col.1030. Cited in *Days of the Lord*, vol. 3, p. 3. [Collegeville: Liturgical Press, 1993]). At the time of Ambrose, the three days were considered to be Friday, Saturday, and Sunday. But by the seventh century a liturgical celebration had been added on Holy Thursday, and the Triduum was considered to start with the Mass of the Lord's Supper.

The liturgy of Holy Thursday allows the symbolic action of washing feet to take place after the homily, but it is important not to see this merely as a historical reenactment of Jesus' action, any more than this or any other celebration of the Eucharist is merely an historical reenactment of the Last Supper. Rather, the liturgy is a commemoration of Jesus' passion, death, and resurrection within the context of a ritual meal. Our theology of liturgy holds that the saving reality of Christ's entire Paschal Mystery is actualized in the celebration and not that this one discrete moment of his

life is rendered present as if in a kind of liturgical passion play. This understanding of how today's celebration is a "memorial" of the Lord's death and resurrection is rooted in the Jewish understanding of *zikkaron* (memorial, or *anamnesis* in Greek). One of the best examples of *zikkaron* is found in the Passover meal, a memorial of the events of the Exodus which in a real way render the saving power of the Lord present in every age. Today's reading from Exodus, describing the origins of the Passover meal, even concludes by saying, "This day shall be a memorial feast for you, which all your generations shall celebrate with pilgrimage to the LORD, as a perpetual institution" (Exodus 12:14). The reading is taken from the narrative of the Tenth Plague into which the sacred author has inserted traditional material describing the rituals that Israel was to observe in remembrance of the events of their liberation from Pharaoh.

The psalm refrain, "Our blessing-cup is a communion with the blood of Christ," is taken from 1 Corinthians and is an appropriate choice given the content of today's second reading. In this part of 1 Corinthians, Paul is emphasizing the traditional nature, "I received from the Lord what I handed on to you" (11:23), of the teaching which the Corinthians were given about the origins and meaning of the eucharistic ritual. Paul's assertion that "every time" they perform this ritual they "proclaim the death of the Lord until he comes" is an excellent example of the continuity of the Jewish notion of *zikkaron* with our Christian understanding that the mystery of the Eucharist is a memorial of the Lord's saving death and resurrection, rendered present to us in every Eucharist.

Today's Gospel helps us understand that every liturgical commemoration also contains an implicit ethical imperative. Jesus tells his disciples that they "must wash each other's feet" and that what he has done is meant as an example for them to follow. Every ritual celebration that is done in memory of Jesus—whether it contains his proclamation of the Gospel, a repetition of his classic actions of taking, blessing, breaking, and sharing, or a symbolic washing of feet—requires that we live in conformity with its meaning. That is why the foundational stories in the Gospels are always so important—because in them are embedded the deep meanings that lie behind the ritual memorials we celebrate. This helps us to see the key role played by today's Johannine text that some scholars feel functions as an equivalent to the institution narrative of the Eucharist that is missing in John but found in all the other Gospels. The meanings that are contained in this Johannine story are all about self-emptying service for the sake of others, redemptive identification with the lowly as a suffering servant, committed discipleship that is willing to share the mission and ministry of Jesus, and a host of other themes that make up the dense content of today's feast.

IMAGES OF PURIFICATION AND ENLIGHTENMENT

Service

Unlike the synoptic accounts which give details of the final Passover supper that Jesus celebrates with his disciples, John's Gospel, while referring to the meal, excludes the details of eating and drinking and focuses instead on another action, washing the disciples' feet. In addition, the evangelist provides both long discourses by Jesus as a kind of final teaching he imparts to them and a prayer for them and for all believers.

Jesus "picked up a towel and tied it around himself" (13:4) and from water poured into a basin, he washes their feet. Then he dries them. Jesus explains this action, saying that while he is indeed Teacher and Lord, he is also Servant. He provides an example and bids his disciples to do as he has done. While the other gospel accounts focus the Passover meal around the words of Jesus which identify the elements of bread and wine with his very person

("Take and eat; this is my body. . . . This is my blood of the covenant. Do this in memory of me"), John's Gospel focuses the Passover meal around the action of washing feet and the example of service Jesus provides. In doing so, heavy emphasis is placed on the notion that eating and drinking the meal of the Lord, the Eucharist, implies willingness to follow the lead of Jesus and serve others.

Believers break open their lives in service to the needs of people, following the example of the Teacher, Lord, and Servant whose own life was offered upon the cross for the sake of the world.

Night and Blood

The first reading contains powerful images from salvation history. As the people of God await their deliverance from slavery in Egypt, each family or group of small families is to slaughter the unblemished, year-old male lamb, put its blood on their doorways, and partake of it that same night. The meal must consist of the whole lamb; that is, it is to be eaten by a community, either by a whole family or, if that family is too small, several families combined together.

It is also a night of judgment. God strikes a blow against the idols of Egypt. The blood on the doorposts and lintels of God's people will mark them out as chosen by heaven, and they will be spared. This is seen by Christians as prefiguring the new covenant established by the blood of Jesus, the Lamb of God who takes away the sins of the world and spares us from destruction.

Handing On

In the second reading Paul explains to the Corinthian community that what he has handed on to them comes from the Lord. Since the days of the early Christian community, a tradition has been handed on in the celebration of the Eucharist. The altar table is set, the gifts of bread and wine are presented, the prayers which reiterate the words of Jesus are spoken and by the grace of God what then is broken, shared, and celebrated is the real presence of Christ, his body and blood.

Generation after generation, from those first times until today, witness to this great mystery of our faith which has been handed on, remembered, proclaimed, and made present. Paul instructs, "Every time, then, you eat this bread and drink this cup, you proclaim the death of the Lord until he comes!" (11:26).

DISMISSAL REFLECTION FOR HOLY THURSDAY

(On this evening the whole session will ordinarily take forty to sixty minutes. This will allow time for the elect and candidates to participate in the community's vigil of prayer.)

Getting Started

Gather in the space that has been prepared ahead of time. Include a pitcher of water, a basin, and a towel. Light the candle and allow quiet time for reflection.

Reflection

1. Lead the group in a reflection on the experience of the liturgy for Holy Thursday. Do this in a meditative fashion. Use these or similar questions, allowing for periods of quiet before proceeding to the next question. Ask such questions as:

   - *What did you observe about tonight's liturgy?* (Pause.) *White vestments . . . The singing of the Gloria . . . The washing of feet . . . Other sights, sounds, smells.*

   - *What words or phrases did you hear?* (Pause.) *"We should glory in the cross of our Lord Jesus Christ." . . . "this month should stand at the head of the calendar." . . . "loins girt, sandals on your feet and your staff in hand, a people in flight" . . . "this is my body" . . . "this is my blood" . . . "do this in memory of me" . . . "begin to wash the disciples' feet" . . . "Do you understand" . . . "then you must wash each other's feet" . . . "as I have done, so you must do" . . . (Pause.)*

   - *What did you hear as the message for the community?*

   - *Who does that message console?*

   - *Who does that message challenge?*

2. Invite them in pairs to share the insights and affirmations and challenges they gained from their reflection. After several minutes, ask each group to share their insights of their discussion with the whole group.

3. Slowly and deliberately proclaim today's Gospel, John 13:1–15. After a few moments of quiet reflection, give each person a copy of Handout 19. Ask the participants to spend the next ten to fifteen minutes privately pondering these questions, which are contained on the handout:

   - Whose feet do I wash?

   - Whose feet do I avoid?

   - Who washes my feet?

   - Who do I refuse to allow to wash my feet?

4. After their time alone, have everyone come back together to share comments on their reflection.

5. Speak briefly about the vigil which is taking place in the parish as you speak. Encourage the elect and candidates to join the parish in keeping vigil this evening. Tell them what time the Good Friday service will be celebrated tomorrow. Then move to brief prayer before joining the rest of the parish in their vigil.

Prayer

Invite everyone to become still, take a few deep breaths, and sing softly several times, "Ubi Caritas" (Taize, GIA Publications, Inc., 1979).

Good Friday
Year A, B, and C

The Celebration of the Lord's Passion

Isaiah 52:13–53:12
Psalm 31:2, 6, 12–13, 15–17, 25
Hebrews 4:14–16; 5:7–9
John 18:1–19:42

The Easter Triduum is, in reality, a single feast; the liturgy of each day of the Triduum celebrates the entire Paschal Mystery (see Holy Thursday in this manual for a full explanation). Good Friday, the "Celebration of the Lord's Passion," focuses on the events that transpired on the day of the Lord's passion and death as a way of understanding and celebrating their meaning in the larger context of the Triduum. Today's liturgy consists of the Liturgy of the Word, the Veneration of the Cross and Holy Communion. The history of the development of these three distinct parts of the Good Friday liturgy is quite diverse, but the most ancient element of the Roman tradition is certainly the Liturgy of the Word with its proclamation of the narrative of the Passion at its heart. The second element, the Veneration of the Cross, was first celebrated in Jerusalem after the discovery of the True Cross, and only later incorporated into liturgies elsewhere in the Christian world. Receiving Holy Communion on this day was sometimes observed and sometimes not, but it was revived in modern times to remind the faithful that Jesus was not "gone" on Good Friday, as was sometimes suggested by a piety focusing on mourning the death of Jesus.

The text from Isaiah is from the fourth Servant-of-the-Lord Song, which is one of a series of poems celebrating a mysterious figure whose vicarious suffering for the people is ultimately redemptive. Christian tradition has from the beginning seen in this text a remarkable foreshadowing of the suffering and death of Jesus. Its influence on the formulation of the gospel accounts of the Passion has long been noted by scholars. It would be hard to overstate the influence of this text on the Christian understanding of the meaning of Christ's death.

The graphic descriptions of the physical sufferings of the Servant make it a natural selection to accompany today's gospel reading. But Isaiah's interpretation of the meaning of the Servant's death "he gives his life as an offering for sin . . . my servant shall justify many, . . . he shall take away the sins of many" (53:10, 11, 12) is even more to the point. The redemptive nature of the Servant's fate is suggested by the author's allusion to the Jewish custom of sacrificing a lamb for the sins of the community: "like a lamb led to the slaughter" (53:7). It is important to note also that the text contains its share of expressions which Christian tradition has seen as allusions to the resurrection: "he shall be raised high and greatly exalted. . . he shall see the light in fullness of days" (52:13; 53-11). Reflective of this, the responsorial psalm proclaims a vision of deep trust in God and peace and confident praise in God's ultimate vindication.

In contrast to Isaiah's unnamed Servant, the reading from Hebrews boldly proclaims the name of him from whom our deliverance has come, "Jesus, the Son of God" (4:14). The text alludes clearly to the human sufferings of Jesus, who "offered prayers and supplications with loud cries and tears" and who "learned obedience from what he suffered" (5:7, 8). It is also unequivocal in its insistence that "when perfected, he became the source of eternal salvation for all who obey him" (5:9). Written to a Jewish Christian community in danger of lapsing from their Christian faith, Hebrews is straightforward in its insistence that "we must hold fast to our profession of faith" if we are to be saved. For a community undergoing the trials of persecution and the temptation to defect, Hebrews has reassuring words of encouragement, urging readers to "confidently approach the throne of grace to receive mercy and favor and to find help in time of need" (4:16).

John's account of the Passion is strikingly different from that of the synoptic gospels. Throughout, John's Gospel portrays Jesus as eager for his "hour" to come. When the time does come, Jesus is shown not merely to submit to his fate but rather to be master of it, freely ascending the cross as if it were a royal throne from which he will rule. The theological themes so carefully woven throughout the earlier chapters of the Gospel all come together in the Passion narrative. Jesus is revealed to be a true king, as the prescription over his head will proclaim and as Pilate is forced to acknowledge. The new Passover lamb willingly offers his life for sinners—just as the lamb is being sacrificed in the Temple. From the cross he gives his mother, the new Eve, to his followers in the person of the beloved disciple. Also from the cross, he breathes forth his spirit in death as if in a new creation of the world, just as the blood and water flowing from his side are seen as the source of the Church's sacramental life. The Johannine account of the Passion seems ideally suited for Good Friday, when the Church celebrates not only the dying of Jesus, but also his glorious triumph in the Resurrection and sending of the Spirit.

IMAGES OF PURIFICATION AND ENLIGHTENMENT

Submission

The words sound like nails being driven into wood; they echo uncomfortably: spurned, stricken, smitten, afflicted, pierced, and crushed. This passage has been described as the fourth song of the Suffering Servant of God. It is not, on its surface, a happy song.

However, it is not without hope. For all of its somber images, Isaiah 52:13–53:12 contains the promise that the Servant of God will suffer in order to assist a divine purpose—the removal of sin and the pardon of many for their offenses. Because of his submission to the divine plan, the Servant, in the end, will be rewarded, "I will give him his portion among the great" (53:12).

Christians see in this passage a direct application to Jesus Christ. The Son of God is the Servant who suffers on behalf of the world, who wins pardon by taking upon himself "the chastisement that makes us whole" (53:5).

Refuge

The psalm text for this Good Friday liturgy complements the first reading, expanding the sense of vindication that is only hinted at in the passage from Isaiah. Hope which is placed in the Lord God will not be disappointed, sings the psalmist. God is a refuge. In spite of adversity and dreadful experiences, life is in the hands of the Most High whose face shines upon God's servants.

Truth

In the Passion narrative of John, the dialogue between Jesus and Pilate is more extensive than that depicted in the synoptic accounts. Pilate is concerned with claims to kingship and power. Jesus responds that his kingdom is not of this world and that he has come to testify to the truth. Pilate scoffs, "Truth! What does that mean?" (18:38). At this point in the narrative, the evangelist does not report what Jesus may have said, if anything was said at all.

But indeed, Jesus has testified to the truth in the passion narrative and the reader knows this truth. It rings loud and clear in the multiple times Jesus reveals his identity, saying, "I am." Three times he responds to those who come to arrest him, "I am." In contrast, when Peter denies him, he does not say, "I do not know him" (as in the Synoptics) but instead he claims, "Not I" (as in "*I am not* one of his followers").

One of the great 'themes' of John's Gospel is identity. In this Gospel, Jesus identifies himself as "I am . . ." the lamb of God, the living water, the light of the world, the shepherd, the sheepgate, the way, the truth, and the life. Peter's denial is all the more damning in that he claims "I am not" follower of the One who proclaims "I am."

This identity theme harks back to the revelation of God to Moses on Sinai "I am who I am" (Exodus 3:14, NAB), and is introduced in the prologue to John's Gospel, "The Word became flesh and made his dwelling among us, and we saw his glory" (John 1:14, NAB). The "truth" of Jesus is God's glory made flesh and revealed among us; the glory of the only Son who goes to the cross for us and bids us, as his disciples, to follow.

The Great High Priest

The second reading from Hebrews also contains some sense of the submission theme found in the passage from Isaiah. Hebrews also contains the image of "high priest" and applies it to Jesus saying, "Christ offered prayers and supplications with loud cries and tears to God" (5:9).

This image in Hebrews—of Jesus, as the great high priest—certainly fits with the Passion narrative from John's Gospel. A very stately Jesus is presented, one who is in command of the events which transpire in Jerusalem. As he hangs dying upon the cross, he commends the disciple to his mother and her to him. At the climactic moment of his death, Jesus proclaims "now it is finished," rather than "breathing his last" as reported in the synoptic Gospels. The account continues "Then he bowed his head, and delivered over his spirit." (19:30).

Jesus truly suffers and dies, and yet, as presented in John's Gospel, he is the Son of God. He is both the victim sacrificed and the high priest making the offering. This is the Good News of salvation.

DISMISSAL REFLECTION FOR GOOD FRIDAY

(On this evening the whole session will ordinarily take forty to sixty minutes.)

Getting Started

Invite everyone to gather in the space that has been prepared ahead of time. Include a large wooden cross. Light the candle and encourage silence. Take the cross and hand it to each person to hold. After everyone has held the cross, sing or play "Behold the Wood" (Dan Schutte, New Dawn Music, 1976).

Reflection

1. Lead everyone in reflecting on their experience of the liturgy of Good Friday. Do this in a meditative style. Ask questions such as these, allowing for periods of quiet before proceeding to the next question.

   - *What did you observe about tonight's liturgy?* (Pause.) *Red vestments . . . The stark environment of the church . . . No entrance song . . . The tenor of the liturgy?* (Pause.)

   - *What did you hear in the Liturgy?* (Pause.) *"Son though he was, he learned obedience from what he suffered." "Give strength to the weary and new courage to those who have lost heart." "Woman, there is your son." "I am thirsty." "Now it is finished." "They looked on him whom they have pierced."* (Pause.)

   - *What is the message proclaimed in tonight's liturgy?*

   - *Who does such a message console?*

   - *Who does such a message challenge?* (Pause.)

2. Invite the participants to share words and phrases, feelings, and observations before asking them to discuss the message of today's liturgy.

3. After a few moments of silence, give each person a copy of Handout 20, which contains these questions:

   - What is the cross in my life?

   - How am I called to embrace the cross?

   - Is my cross a cross of suffering or a cross of victory?

   Ask everyone to spend the next fifteen to twenty minutes privately pondering the questions.

4. After spending time privately reflecting on the questions, call everyone back together to share comments on their reflections.

5. Summarize their comments and reflections, stressing that in embracing the cross, we are participating in the ongoing Paschal Mystery of Jesus Christ.

Prayer

Invite everyone to become still by taking a few deep breaths. Hand the cross to each person, one at a time, again. Sing "Lift High the Cross" (Text: George W. Kitchin and Michael R. Newbott. Tune: CRUCIFER, 10 10 with refrain; Sydney H. Nicholson, Hope Publishing Co., 1978).

Chapter 5
Scrutiny and Penitential Rite Preparation

Introduction

This chapter contains sessions to be used as preparation for the three Scrutinies celebrated with the elect and/or the Penitential Rite celebrated with the baptized candidates. The sessions are designed to incorporate members of the parish as well as the elect with their godparents and the candidates with their sponsors. The Scripture readings for the sessions are the lectionary readings for the particular Sunday on which the Rite will be celebrated. For the sake of variety, two alternatives are provided for each Sunday; for the Third Sunday of Lent (First Scrutiny), three choices are offered. Any of these alternatives may be chosen, depending on the needs of the group.

In these sessions, the participants are engaged in a reflective process to name particular manifestations of what the Rite of Christian Initiation of Adults calls "the mystery of sin, from which the whole world and every person longs to be delivered" (RCIA, 143). The manifestations of sin named, which may range from personal demons to the great social ills and evils that disfigure human life on a large scale, will be used in crafting the intercessions for the upcoming Penitential Rite or Rite of Scrutiny.

At the conclusion of each of the preparation sessions, the catechist collects what has been named and works with the pastor, liturgist, and musician in order to incorporate the list into the Scrutiny or Penitential Rite. The intercessions given in the ritual text (RCIA, 153) are thus adapted in order "to fit the various circumstances" of the elect, candidates, and assembly (RCIA, 153, 167, 174).

The preparation sessions are ordinarily held during the week preceding the Rite. The space is prepared ahead of time. The chairs are arranged in groups of four or six. The focal point of the room is a table draped with a purple cloth on which is set a candle and the Lectionary opened to the appropriate Sunday's readings. For certain weeks an additional symbol is suggested.

Ordinarily the sessions will take sixty to ninety minutes. The pace of the sessions is reflective and deliberate, allowing for periods of interior recollection. It is necessary to allow enough time for personal struggles not only to surface but also for the participants to begin to identify and grapple with the larger, deeper struggles of societal and systemic sin.

Participation in the liturgical experience of the Scrutiny or Penitential Rite—either as elect or baptized candidates or as members of the assembly—brings to a certain fulfillment the process that the preparation session begins. It is important to remember that these sessions are incomplete without the celebration of liturgical rites which bring to solemn community prayer the concerns raised in them.

Likewise, each reflection and celebration is designed to draw forth a progressively deeper awareness of the mystery of sin and grace, week by week. The movement undertaken in these preparation sessions and in the Scrutinies is not complete in itself but leads to the celebration of the Easter Vigil—where sin is renounced in all its forms, and Christ's victory over sin and death embraces us at font and holy table.

This preparation occurs prior to the celebration of the Penitential Rite for candidates, preferably early in the week preceding the Second Sunday of Lent. The candidates and their sponsors, members of the team, and members of the parish gather for this preparation (see Chapter 3: The Parish). Elect and their godparents may also attend.

Gathering

1. Prepare the room by arranging small circles of four or six chairs. Place the Lectionary on a table in a prominent place in the room. Have the table draped in purple, with a candle placed on it.

2. Welcome everyone. Invite the participants to be seated in groups, with the candidates seated with their sponsors. Begin by saying briefly these or similar words:

   We are in the midst of the season of Lent. Lent offers us the opportunity to step back from the busyness of our lives to examine our relationship with God, people, and things. In doing so, it is important to name the places of struggle in these relationships, to name what keeps us and our communities and our society from living in a right relationship with God, people, and things. The task for this session is to prepare for the ritual celebration which will take place next Sunday. Part of the preparation is to name what is at the heart of our struggles and to bring it to prayer.

Prayer

1. Invite the participants to close their eyes and take several deep breaths, breathing out the tiredness or stresses of the day and breathing in the freshness of God's presence.

2. Light the candle.

3. Sing "Transform Us" (lyrics by Sylvia Dunstan, music by Richard Proulx, GIA Publications, Inc., 1986, 1993).

4. Pray in these or words of your own:

   Good and gracious God,
   we give thanks and praise to you for the gift of
   *   your Son, Jesus Christ,*
   who freely chose to die for our redemption.
   As we gather to reflect on our lives, our
   *   communities, and our society, and*
   to discern how we are doing as his disciples,
   we ask you to send your Spirit to be with us, to
   *   strengthen us and to lead us in this reflection.*
   We trust in your promise to be with us always.
   We ask this in the name of Jesus. Amen.

Reflection

1. Proclaim 2 Timothy 1:8–10, the second reading for the Second Sunday of Lent, Year A.

2. After a few moments of silence, ask the participants to ponder this sentence: Bear your share of the hardship which the Gospel entails (2 Timothy 1:8). Invite them to name the following:

   - the places in our world, society, and neighborhoods where they observe that living the gospel commandments to love God and to love neighbor is a hardship, and

   - the causes of hardship in living the Gospel.

   (Have a team member write the responses down on paper so that they can be used in adapting the litany of intercession for the Penitential Rite on Sunday.)

3. Ask the participants to share in pairs (candidate with sponsor, and others paired however they wish) the ways in which they experience hardship in trying to live the Gospel. Give them fifteen to twenty minutes for this sharing.

4. Gather everyone back together. Invite the pairs to give a summary of their sharing. Write the hardships each pair names on newsprint, the chalkboard, or an overhead transparency.

5. Explain that on Sunday the parish community will gather with the candidates in a special way to pray with and for them as they continue the journey of faith leading them to complete their Christian initiation or to be received into the full communion of the Catholic Church at the Easter Vigil.

   Invite everyone to stand. Ask the sponsors to stand behind their candidates and put their hands on the shoulders of their candidates. Pray in these or similar words:

   God, you have called us your sons and daughters.
   Embrace and strengthen these candidates as they
   *   journey to the eucharistic table*
   where they will be nourished with the body and
   *   blood of Christ.*
   Keep these chosen ones safe in your love.
   We ask this in the name of Jesus Christ, who lives
   *   and reigns with you and the Holy Spirit, one*
   *   God, forever and ever. Amen.*

Closing

Conclude by singing "Transform Us" again.

This preparation occurs prior to the celebration of the Penitential Rite, preferably during the week preceding the Second Sunday of Lent. The candidates and their sponsors, members of the team, and members of the parish gather for this preparation (see Chapter 3: The Parish). Elect and their godparents may also attend.

Gathering

1. Prepare the room by arranging small circles of four or six chairs. The Lectionary, opened to the readings for the Second Sunday of Lent, is placed on a table, which is located in a prominent place in the room. The table, draped in purple, has a lighted candle on it.

2. Welcome everyone. Invite the participants to be seated in groups, with the candidates seated with their sponsors. Begin by saying briefly these or similar words:

   We are in the midst of the season of Lent. Lent offers us the opportunity to step back from the busyness of our lives to examine our relationship with God, people, and things. In doing so, it is important to name the places of struggle in these relationships, to name what keeps us and our communities and our society from living in a right relationship with God, people, and things. The task for this session is to prepare for the ritual celebration which will take place next Sunday. Part of the preparation is to name what is at the heart of our struggles and to bring it to prayer.

Prayer

1. Invite the participants to close their eyes and take several deep breaths, breathing out the tiredness or stresses of the day and breathing in the freshness of God's presence.

2. Light the candle.

3. Sing "Psalm 97: The Lord is King" (The Grail, GIA Publications, Inc., 1993).

4. Pray in these or words of your own:

   God, you are the Creator of all life.
   We give thanks and praise to you for the gift of
       your Son, Jesus Christ,
   who freely chose to die for our redemption.
   As we gather to reflect on our lives, our
       communities, and our society,
   and to discern how we are doing as his disciples,
   we ask you to send your Spirit to be with us and to
       strengthen us, and to lead us in this reflection.
   We trust in your promise to be with us always.
   We ask this in the name of Jesus. Amen.

Reflection

1. Thoughtfully and deliberately proclaim Matthew 17:1–9, the Gospel for Second Sunday of Lent.

2. Lead the participants in the following meditation:

   Close your eyes. Imagine you are at the base of a mountain. (Pause.) You look up and see a path ascending the mountain. You begin to walk the path. (Pause.) Part way up the mountain, Jesus joins you and the two of you continue to climb, talking about things that you have been pondering in your heart. (Long pause.) As you near the top, Jesus speaks to you about the glory that awaits all his disciples. (Pause.) At the top of the mountain, the two of you survey the beauty of all creation which surrounds you. It is indeed breathtaking. Jesus says to you that you are his chosen one in whom he is pleased. You bow your head as you reflect on the struggles you experience in being Jesus' disciple. (Pause.) You speak to Jesus about these struggles and you ask for forgiveness and the strength to change those attitudes, prejudices, and actions which are not those of a disciple. (Pause.) Jesus embraces you. (Pause.) Slowly, the two of you begin the journey down the mountain. Jesus speaks to you about living in the world as his disciple. He assures you that his grace is enough for you if only you ask for it. He reminds you that you are not alone—that you need to keep good company, particularly the community of faith. (Pause.) You have reached the spot where Jesus joined you. As he leaves he blesses you. You continue down the mountain. (Pause.)

3. Invite the participants to open their eyes. Ask the candidates and sponsors to join in pairs (with other participants pairing up as they wish) and to share what meaning this meditation has for them.

4. After twenty minutes or so, distribute a piece of paper to each participant, and ask them to write the name of the struggle or struggles they discussed in their conversation with Jesus.

5. Collect these papers. Explain that the struggles will be incorporated into the Penitential Rite for this coming Sunday.

   Invite everyone to stand. Ask the sponsors to stand behind their candidates and put their hands on the shoulders of their candidates. Pray in these or similar words:

   God, you have called us your sons and daughters.
   Embrace and strengthen these candidates as they
       journey to the eucharistic table
   where they will be nourished with the body and
       blood of Christ.
   Keep these chosen ones safe in your love. We ask
       this in the name of Jesus Christ, who lives and
       reigns with you and the Holy Spirit, one God,
       forever and ever. Amen.

Closing

Conclude by singing "You Are Mine" (David Haas, GIA Publications, Inc., 1991).

PREPARATION FOR THE FIRST SCRUTINY, THIRD SUNDAY OF LENT: OPTION 1

This preparation occurs prior to the celebration of the First Scrutiny on the Third Sunday of Lent, preferably early in the week preceding the celebration. The elect, godparents, candidates, sponsors, and members of the team participate. All members of the parish may also be invited to participate in such a preparation (see Chapter 3: The Parish).

Gathering

1. Prepare the room by arranging small circles of four or six chairs. The Lectionary, opened to the Third Sunday of Lent, is placed on a table, which is located in a prominent place in the room. The table, draped with a purple cloth, has a lighted candle on it as well.

2. Welcome everyone. Acknowledge those who were present last week, and warmly welcome any newcomers. Invite the participants to be seated in groups, with the elect and candidates seated with their godparents and sponsors. If there are newcomers, allow some time for people to introduce themselves to one another in their small groups. Begin by saying briefly these or similar words:

   We gather again today, as we did last week, to reflect on our lives as we prepare for a ritual that we will experience next Sunday.

   We are in the midst of the season of Lent. Lent offers us the opportunity to step back from the busyness of our lives to examine our relationship with God, people, and things. In doing so, it is important to name the places of struggle in these relationships, to name what keeps us and our communities and our society from living in a right relationship with God, people, and things. The task for this session is to prepare for the ritual celebration which will take place next Sunday. Part of the preparation is to name what is at the heart of our struggles and bring it to prayer.

Prayer

1. Invite the participants to close their eyes and to take several deep breaths, breathing out the tiredness or stresses of the day and breathing in the freshness of God's presence.

2. Chant several times "Jesus Remember Me" (Les Presses de Taize, France, 1981).

3. Pray in these or words of your own:
   Good and gracious God,
   we gather to reflect on our lives, our communities, and our society,
   and to discern how we are responding to your call to be disciples of your Son, Jesus Christ. Send your Spirit to be with us, and to strengthen us, to lead us in this reflection.
   We trust in your promise to be with us always.
   We pray this in the name of Jesus, our brother. Amen.

Reflection

1. Proclaim Exodus 17:3–7 the first reading for the Third Sunday of Lent.

2. After a few minutes of silence say:
   The Israelites are outcasts in the desert. They do not belong anywhere; certainly they cannot go back to Egypt. They are not yet in the Promised Land. Literally, they are thirsting for water, but truly their thirsts are much deeper. They thirst for a deeper faith and trust in God's promise of a new homeland, a place flowing with milk and honey.

3. Proclaim Exodus 17:3–7 again. After a few moments of silence, ask everyone to think about the following: Who are the outcasts in our world? In our society? In our communities? What do they thirst for? After several minutes of silent reflection, have them work in small groups and name today's outcasts and their thirsts. When you think the groups are ready, call them back together by singing "Jesus Remember Me" several times. Invite each group to name the people they named as outcasts and to list their thirsts. Have someone record the group's responses on newsprint, on the chalkboard, or on a piece of paper.

4. Lead the discussion to a new dimension by asking volunteers to name what causes people to remain outcasts. Begin by asking, What keeps the outcasts from coming to the source of water to which everyone has a right? After a few minutes of quiet reflection invite everyone to share in their groups the causes of separation and isolation that they identified in their reflections. When they have had some time to share, call them back together by singing several times "Jesus Remember Me." Then invite each small group to share their responses aloud with the whole group. Have someone record these responses as above.

5. Proclaim Exodus 17:3–7 a third time. Now ask the participants to reflect on their own lives. Lead the reflection by asking:
   - In what way have you experienced being an outcast and what was the cause?
   - Who have you made an outcast and for what reason?
   - What keeps you and others from the water which would quench your thirst?

6. After several minutes, invite everyone to share in their groups the insights they gained from the reflection. (Give everyone a pencil and piece of paper on which to write down the causes or reasons and collect them in a basket after they have had some quiet time to write the insights they gained.)

7. Encourage all to continue during the week to reflect on Exodus 17:3–7 in preparation for the coming Sunday. Ask them to include in their reflection the many ways in which God has already quenched their thirsts.

Closing

Invite all to stand in their small groups and share spontaneous prayer or quiet prayer together. After all have had time to do this, chant several times "Jesus Remember Me."

This preparation occurs prior to the celebration of the First Scrutiny on the Third Sunday of Lent, preferably early in the week preceding the celebration. The elect, godparents, candidates, sponsors, and members of the team participate. All members of the parish may also be invited to participate in such a preparation (see Chapter 3: The Parish).

Gathering

1. Prepare the room by arranging small circles of four or six chairs. The Lectionary, opened to the Third Sunday of Lent, is placed on a table which is located in a prominent place in the room. The table, draped in purple, has a lighted candle and an empty basket on it.

2. Welcome everyone. If a similar gathering was held the week before, acknowledge those who have come a second time, and warmly welcome any newcomers. Invite the participants to be seated in groups, with the elect and candidates seated with their godparents and sponsors. Begin by saying briefly these or similar words:

   We gather again today, as we did last week, to reflect on our lives in preparation for the ritual we will experience next Sunday.

   We are in the midst of the season of Lent. Lent offers us the opportunity to step back from the busyness of our lives to examine our relationship with God, people, and things. In doing so, it is important to name the places of struggle in these relationships, to name what keeps us and our communities and our society from living in right relationship with God, people, and things. The task for this session is to prepare for the ritual celebration which will take place next Sunday. Part of the preparation is to name what is at the heart of our struggles and to bring it to prayer.

Prayer

1. Invite the participants to close their eyes and take several deep breaths, breathing out the tiredness or stresses of the day and breathing in the freshness of God's presence.

2. Sing "Come to the Water" (John B. Foley, New Dawn Music, 1978).

3. Pray in these or words of your own:

   Good and gracious God,
   we gather to reflect on our lives, our communities, and our society
   and to discern how we are responding to the call to be disciples of your Son, Jesus Christ.
   Send your Spirit to be with us, to strengthen us and to lead us in this reflection.
   We trust in your promise to be with us always.
   We pray this in the name of Jesus, our brother. Amen.

Reflection

1. Proclaim John 4:5–18.

2. After a few minutes of silent reflection, say in these or your own words:

   Jesus is talking with a woman who is also a Samaritan. This is certainly a surprise to her. Samaritans worshiped false gods, so good Jewish people were expected to avoid Samaritans. Yet Jesus does speak to her and reveals many things to her about himself and about herself. Some Scripture scholars have interpreted the dialogue about the woman's five husbands to be a discussion about worship and false gods. In Hebrew the word ba'al *means husband. Perhaps Jesus' comments about the woman's five husbands is a reference to the five idols (false gods) which the Jews of Samaria adopted into their faith.*

3. Proclaim John 4:5–18 again. After several moments of silence, ask everyone to think about: Who or what are the false gods or idols of our world, society, and community which take us away from the one true God?

4. Allow sufficient time for quiet reflection, then ask the small groups to name the false gods or idols that they have identified. Encourage them to discuss why it is difficult to recognize such false gods or idols in our surroundings.

5. After ten to fifteen minutes of small group discussion, call the participants back together by singing several times the first line of "Come to the Water." Invite each small group to share with the whole groups what they identified as the false gods or idols of our world, of our society, and of our community. Have someone write down what each group names on newsprint, chalkboard, or paper.

6. Proclaim again John 4:5–18. Now ask everyone to individually reflect on their own lives and to name the false gods or idols that are present in their own lives. Encourage the participants to think about what keeps them from putting God at the center of their lives.

7. Distribute to everyone a piece of paper and a pencil. Invite them to write down the false gods or idols present in their lives, and to fold the paper when they are done.

8. Proclaim John 4:7–15. After a few moments of silence, invite everyone to come forward, one by one, and place their folded piece of paper in the basket on the table. Sing or play "Come to the Water" until all have placed their papers in the basket.

Closing

After everyone has returned to their places, invite them to pray together in their small groups. After all have had time to pray, sing the refrain again. Remind the participants that they are preparing for the Rite of Scrutiny which they will celebrate this coming Sunday. Encourage them to continue to reflect on the many ways that they are distracted from the love of God and the love of neighbor. Encourage them also to give thanks to God for the many blessings that each of them has received from a loving God, who is always forgiving.

This preparation occurs prior to the celebration of the First Scrutiny on the Third Sunday of Lent, preferably early in the week preceding the celebration. The elect, godparents, candidates, sponsors, and members of the team participate. All members of the parish may also be invited to participate in such a preparation (see Chapter 3: The Parish).

Gathering

1. Prepare the room by arranging small circles of four or six chairs. The Lectionary, opened to the Third Sunday of Lent, is placed on a table which is located in a prominent place in the room. The table, draped with a purple cloth, has a lighted candle on it. An empty water jar may also be placed on or near the table.

2. Welcome everyone. If a similar gathering was held the week before, acknowledge those who have come a second time, and warmly welcome any newcomers. Invite the participants to be seated in groups with the elect and candidates seated with their godparents and sponsors. If there are newcomers, allow some time for people to introduce themselves to one another Begin by saying briefly these or similar words:

   We gather again today, as we did last week, to reflect on our lives in preparation for the ritual we will experience next Sunday.

   We are in the midst of the season of Lent. Lent offers us the opportunity to step back from the busyness of our lives to examine our relationship with God, people, and things. In doing so, it is important to name the places of struggle in these relationships, to name what keeps us and, our communities and our society from living in a right relationship with God, people, and things. The task for this session is to prepare for the ritual celebration which will take place next Sunday. Part of the preparation is to name what is at the heart of our struggles and to bring it to prayer.

Prayer

1. Invite the participants to close their eyes and take several deep breaths, breathing out the tiredness or stresses of the day and breathing in the freshness of God's presence.

2. Chant several times "Give Us Living Water" (David Haas, *Who Calls You By Name*, Vol II, GIA Publications, Inc., 1988.

3. Pray in these or words of your own:

   Good and gracious God,
   we gather to reflect on our lives, our communities,
   *   and our society*
   and to discern how we are responding to your call
   *   to be disciples of your Son, Jesus Christ.*
   Send your Spirit to be with us and to strengthen us,
   *   to lead us in this reflection.*
   We trust in your promise to be with us always.
   We pray this in the name of Jesus, our brother. Amen.

Reflection

1. Proclaim Exodus 17:3–7.

2. Invite participants to close their eyes. Read this poetic reflection very slowly and deliberately:

   Come with me as I sit on my patio
   There among coleus and hibiscus, among
   *   geraniums and spruce,*
   among vines of vinca and pots of portulaca,
   There, in five-gallon buckets, see the miracle that
   *   I see.*
   My tomato plants!
   Sprung from the seeds of summer past
   birthed amid March winds and winter snows,
   green and still
   covered in morning dew, caressed in cool amber
   *   light:*
   bud and blossom, tiny fruit and green, full fruit,
   *   red and firm,*
   bursting with sweetness, "delightful to look at and
   *   good for food"*
   gift of sun and earth and water.
   But we cannot linger for long,
   and so we leave my stockade-fenced Eden and go
   *   about our day.*

Later, the sun presses on to its zenith

*it leaps over the corner of the house and engulfs
  the patio with blinding force;*

the slate bakes in foot-searing heat;

eyes burn and smart as the sun shimmers

in the arid emptiness of summer day noontime.

The branches of those tomatoes,

so strong and vibrant in the new day's coolness

*now droop under the glare of the sun and the
  weight of their fruit,*

dusty and no longer so brilliantly red.

Their tiniest leaves almost steamed to death.

*Their roots stretch out in vain for the moisture that
  would save them,*

*with the garden hose lying limp and idle and so
  ineffectual, so nearby.*

*The sun stands still in agonizing and seemingly
  endless noontime,*

its light and heat continue their relentless glare

to wither, to scorch, to parch.

A strange thing—and sad—that thirst

can so rob living things of their being,

can so wear down strength to weakness,

can so parch fruitfulness to barrenness

can turn life, slowly and agonizingly,

to death.

*Is it any wonder then that the Evil One tempts Jesus
  in the desert?*

A place scorched by the sun,

a place parched by the heat,

*a place made barren for lack of life-giving water—
  a place of thirst?*

*People journey tempted through a sometimes desert
  of life—thirsting for hope and understanding*

thirsting for recognition and justice,

thirsting for equality and dignity,

thirsting for truth and goodness,

thirsting for fidelity and peace,

thirsting for holiness and life,

thirsting for all these and more,

afraid of dying of thirst.

Andy Varga, 1990. Used with permission.

3. Sing "Give Us Living Water" again, several times.

4. Speak the following:

   *If thirsting hearts and parched lives are to be
   quenched, we must stand firm and allow everyone
   to come to the well of life-giving waters. In the presence of the power of Jesus, the Living Water, the
   thirsts must be named. Whatever keeps people from
   access to the well of living water must be named so
   that Jesus might destroy the evil forever.*

5. Invite everyone to work in their small groups to name
   (a) what people are thirsting for and (b) the forces of
   evil which keep them from having their thirst
   quenched by the living water. Have each group
   record on paper the thirsts and the forces of evil
   which keep people from having their thirsts
   quenched.

6. After everyone has had time to finish, call them back
   together by singing "Give Us Living Water" several times.

7. Collect the papers from each group.

Closing

1. Encourage everyone to continue, throughout the
   week, to reflect on both their thirsts for living water
   and also on what keeps them from having their thirsts
   quenched. Tell them that this Sunday we will celebrate the Rite of Scrutiny and that the thirsts and
   forces of evil they named this evening will be part of
   the prayer. Invite all to stand in their small groups
   and pray together. After all have had time to pray,
   lead everyone in singing "Give Us Living Water."

PREPARATION FOR THE SECOND SCRUTINY, FOURTH SUNDAY OF LENT: OPTION 1

This preparation occurs prior to the celebration of the Second Scrutiny on the Fourth Sunday of Lent, preferably early in the week preceding the celebration. The elect, godparents, candidates, sponsors, and members of the team participate. All members of the parish may also be invited to take part in such a preparation (see Chapter 3: The Parish).

Gathering

1. Prepare the room by arranging small circles of four or six chairs. On a purple-draped table, in a prominent place in the room, rests the Lectionary opened to the Fourth Sunday of Lent. A basket and candle are also on the table.

2. Welcome everyone and allow time for newcomers to introduce themselves. Invite the participants to be seated in small groups, with the elect and candidates seated with their godparents and sponsors. Begin by saying briefly these or similar words:

   Last week we reflected on our thirsts and the living water offered to the world by Jesus. This week, we delve more deeply into the mystery of sin and God's love for us by asking where we, as individuals and communities, are very much in darkness and so greatly need the light of Christ. It is important to look, and look again, at our experiences and name the places of struggle in our relationship with God, people, and things. We are here tonight to ask God to reveal to us what keeps us, our communities, and our society from living the light of Christ. The task for this session is to prepare for the ritual celebration which will take place next Sunday. Part of the preparation is to name what is at the heart of our struggles and bring it to prayer.

Prayer

1. Light the candle and invite the participants to close their eyes and take several deep breaths, breathing out the tiredness or stresses of the day and breathing in the freshness of God's presence.

2. Pray in these or words of your own:

   Good and gracious God,
   we gather to reflect on our lives, our communities, and our society,
   and to discern how we are responding to your call to live as disciples of your Son, Jesus Christ.
   Send your Spirit to be with us, to strengthen us, and to lead us in this reflection.
   We trust in your promise to be with us always.
   We pray this in the name of Jesus, our brother.
   Amen.

Reflection

1. Proclaim Ephesians 5:8–14, which is the second reading for the Fourth Sunday of Lent, Year A.

2. Invite everyone to close their eyes. Then lead them in this reflection:

   Imagine a world in which all are living as children of light as God desires. (Pause.) *Imagine the workplace.* (Pause.) *Imagine the world in which everyone has enough food and clothing and a home and a job.* (Pause.)

   After a few minutes of silent reflection, invite them to share what they imagined.

3. In five minutes, with the whole group, share comments and reflections aloud.

4. Proclaim Ephesians 5:8–14 again.

5. Ask them to work in their groups to describe what "pleases the Lord" (Ephesians 5:10).

6. After a few minutes' discussion, gather comments and insights from each small group.

7. Ask everyone to ponder these questions:

   - What are the fruitless works of darkness in our world, our society, and our communities that need to be exposed in the light of Jesus, who is the truth?

   - What keeps us from living as children of light?

   After a few moments of quiet reflection, have them discuss responses to the two questions in their small groups, with one member of each group recording the responses. Give the groups fifteen to twenty minutes for this activity. Invite the recorder to share the results of the discussion.

8. Proclaim Ephesians 5:8–14 a third time.

9. After a moment of silent reflection, give everyone a piece of paper and have each participant write on it one fruitless work of darkness from which he or she would like to be delivered. When the participants are ready, invite them to place the pieces of paper in the basket on the table.

10. Proclaim John 9:1–41, the Gospel for the Fourth Sunday of Lent. You might play a recording of this Gospel done by David Haas (*Who Calls You By Name*, GIA Publications, Inc., 1988).

11. After a few moments of quiet reflection, spend some time naming the many gifts you have been given by Jesus Christ, who is the Light of the world.

Closing

Invite all to stand in their small groups and to share a spontaneous or quiet prayer together. After all have had time to pray, sing an appropriate song such as "We Are Marching" (Ultryck, *Ritual Song*, GIA Publications, Inc., 1996) or "We Are The Light of the World" (Vernacular Hymns Publishing Co., 1966).

PREPARATION FOR THE SECOND SCRUTINY, FOURTH SUNDAY OF LENT: OPTION 2

This preparation occurs prior to the celebration of the Second Scrutiny on the Fourth Sunday of Lent, preferably early in the week preceding the celebration. The elect, godparents, candidates, sponsors, and members of the team participate. All members of the parish may also be invited to take part in such a preparation (see Chapter 3: The Parish).

Gathering

1. Prepare the room by arranging small circles of four or six chairs. On a purple-draped table in a prominent place in the room rests the Lectionary, opened to the Fourth Sunday of Lent. A basket and candle are also on the table.

2. Welcome everyone and allow time for newcomers to introduce themselves. Invite the participants to be seated in small groups, with the elect and candidates seated with their godparents and sponsors. Begin by saying briefly these or similar words:

   Last week we reflected on our thirsts and the living water offered to the world by Jesus. This week, we delve more deeply into the mystery of sin and God's love for us by asking where we, as individuals and communities, are very much in darkness and so greatly need the light of Christ. It is important to look, and look again, at our experiences and name the places of struggle in our relationship with God, people and things. We are here tonight to ask God to reveal to us what keeps us, our communities, and our society from living in the light of Christ. The task for this session is to prepare for the ritual celebration which will take place next Sunday. Part of the preparation is to name what is at the heart of our struggles and bring it to prayer.

Prayer

1. Invite everyone to close their eyes and take several deep breaths, breathing out the tiredness or stresses of the day and breathing in the freshness of God's presence.

2. Chant several times "The Lord is my Light and my Salvation" (David Haas, GIA Publications, Inc., 1983).

Reflection

1. Proclaim Ephesians 5:8–14 thoughtfully and deliberately, followed by several moments of silence.

2. Lead the group in a reflection with these or similar words:

   Have you ever watched nightfall in a setting not affected by artificial light or pollution? (Pause.) Journey with me into the desert for a few moments. Imagine yourself sitting outdoors, surrounded by the desert sands. Imagine the boulders strewn about by the mighty hand of nature. Notice the life of the desert; its flowers, the plants, and its living creatures. Now, feel the warmth of the sand beginning to fade as the sun descends. The sun's light dims, fades, and slowly disappears. Colors lose their power and everything becomes a shade of grey. Darkness begins to fill up first tiny crevices, then wide spaces; it floods great chasm with its inky, liquid blackness. It surrounds. It invades. It pervades. It penetrates all that is. (Pause.) Is it any wonder that the Evil One is called the Prince of Darkness? Darkness which at first surrounds us, comforts us, tempts us. (Pause.)

   Darkness which then pervades the imagination . . .

   invades the intellect . . .

   penetrates the heart . . .

   Darkness which blurs the vision, destroys the sight, creates a blindness:

   Blindness to good . . .

   Blindness to truth . . .

   Blindness to value . . .

   Blindness to beauty . . .

   Blindness to thought . . .

   Blindness to holiness . . .

   Blindness to love . . .

   Blindness to live itself . . .

   Sadly, darkness and blindness which are tolerated and sometimes chosen.

   Poetic reflection written by Andy Varga, 1990.
   Used with permission.

3. After several minutes of quiet reflection, begin humming "Amazing Grace." Then continue by saying:

   If the darkness is to become light, we must look to Jesus, the Light. The darkness must be named in the light of God's Spirit.

4. Invite everyone, while remaining in their small groups, to peer into our world, both secular and ecclesial, and to search its systems and politics, its protocols and prejudices, its attitudes and presumptions, and point out where they see the darkness pervading and penetrating, blurring our vision, and causing our blindness. Ask them to name what causes such darkness and blindness in our world. Have one person in each group act as a recorder, writing down these examples of darkness and blindness, so that the examples they name can become part of the Rite of Scrutiny on Sunday. After fifteen to twenty minutes, collect the papers from the groups.

Closing

Invite all to stand in their small groups and pray together, either spontaneously or quietly. After all have had time to pray, sing "Amazing Grace" together.

PREPARATION FOR THE THIRD SCRUTINY, FIFTH SUNDAY OF LENT: OPTION 1

This preparation occurs prior to the celebration of the Third Scrutiny on the Fifth Sunday of Lent, preferably early in the week preceding the celebration. The elect, godparents, candidates, sponsors, and members of the team participate. All members of the parish may also be invited to participate in such a preparation (see Chapter 3: The Parish).

Gathering

1. Prepare the room by arranging small circles of four or six chairs. The Lectionary, opened to the Fifth Sunday of Lent, along with a lighted candle, is placed on a table in a prominent place in the room. The table is draped with a purple cloth.

2. Welcome the participants and allow time for newcomers to be introduced. Invite everyone to be seated in small groups, with the elect and candidates seated with their godparents and sponsors. Begin by stating briefly these or similar words:

   Each week that we celebrate the Rite of Scrutiny, as we have for the past two Sundays during Lent, we are invited deeper and deeper into a great mystery that affects all people. Our world is thirsting, we are thirsting, and Jesus brings us living water. Our world is blind, we are blind, and Jesus opens our eyes. Today we take one step further on our Lenten journey as we open up the Scriptures for the Fifth Sunday of Lent and our lives in reflection and prayer. Tonight we will name what keeps us, our communities, and our society from the abundant life that God wants us to have. The task for this session is to prepare for the ritual celebration which will take place next Sunday: the last of the three Scrutinies. Part of our preparation is to name what we know to be death and to bring it to prayer.

Prayer

1. Invite everyone to close their eyes and take several deep breaths, breathing out the tiredness or stresses of the day and breathing in the freshness of God's presence.

2. Pray in these or words of your own:

   Good and gracious God,
   we gather to reflect on our lives, our communities, and our society,
   and to discern how we are responding to your call to be disciples of your Son, Jesus Christ.
   Send your Spirit to be with us, to strengthen us and to lead us in this reflection.
   We trust in your promise to be with us always.
   We pray this in the name of Jesus, our brother. Amen.

Reflection

1. Proclaim Ezekiel 37:1–14, thoughtfully and deliberately.

2. After several minutes of silence, invite everyone to close their eyes and imagine that they are in a cemetery. Allow time for people to enter into this reflection, then continue with these or similar words:

   It is November; the sky is dark . . . and grey . . . and cold . . .
   Thick clouds rush by, low and menacing, almost touching the top of a car, smelling almost of snow.
   The winds that move clouds along carry wide swaths of dried leaves, rustling by in swirls of brown.
   And there, on some oak trees, other dry leaves are sentenced to cling to their branches all winter long, constantly whispering a mournful memory of last summer's demise.
   Your eyes wander to another reminder of death;
   the row upon row upon row of headstones,
   standing large and small, ornate and plain,
   some etched razor sharp, some weathered dull and crumbling, black and white and every shade of grey in their array diagonal, perhaps already long-forgotten by those who built them in "everlasting" memory.

But still, these granite and marble sentinels stand . . .

Silently watching,

silently guarding,

silently naming,

those who have gone before us;

those who await us.

*Here and there, mounds of browning flowers,
plastic baskets,*

*relational ribbons soaked and sodden with
autumn rain,*

*reminder of recent grief, hidden from sight, but
still too tender to touch,*

*temporary blanket of tribute for the soon-to-be
dried bones beneath.*

The stones . . . the bones . . .

The sky . . . the leaves . . .

The rustle . . . the rain . . .

*The radio . . . it plays a modern-day Qoheleth's
chant . . .*

It is clear and so painfully true;

*no leaf, no flower, no fish, no fowl, no beast, nor
mighty tree or flinty stone*

no woman, no man

nothing created escapes the grasp of death.

*Is it any wonder, then, that the Evil One is called
the Prince of Death?*

Death which comes great

Death which comes small

*Death which comes in every conceivable form; in
the passing of time and season, in waiting and
weakness, in sorrow and surrender;*

*death which weighs down like massive granite
slabs upon the dried ones of all the world
ponderous stones sealing humanity in tombs of
poverty, and disease, ignorance, indifference;
wrapped in winding-sheet stench of bias and
hatred and violence,*

*death which tempts and touches and tortures us
again and again and again until death.*

> Poetic reflection written by Andy Varga, 1990.
> Used with permission.

3. After several minutes of quiet reflection, continue with these or similar words:

> *If death is to become life, we must turn to Jesus who is the Resurrection and the Life. Death must be faced in the power of him who conquered all death by his own dying.*

4. Invite everyone, remaining in their small groups, to peer into our world, both secular and ecclesial, and point out where they see the power of death at work.

5. Allow some time for small group discussions, then invite the groups to share what they discussed with the whole group. Write the results of their discussion on newsprint, chalkboard, or on an overhead transparency for all to see. If there is not enough time for the large group sharing, ask each group to choose a recorder to write down the results of their discussion and give it to you before they leave. Tell the participants that what has been written down will be used in the Scrutiny to be celebrated on Sunday.

Closing

Chant "God of the Living, Not of the Dead" (David Haas, GIA Publications, Inc., 1988) several times.

PREPARATION FOR THE THIRD SCRUTINY, FIFTH SUNDAY OF LENT: OPTION 2

This preparation occurs prior to the celebration of the Third Scrutiny on the Fifth Sunday of Lent, preferably early in the week preceding the celebration. The elect, godparents, candidates, sponsors, and members of the team participate. All members of the parish may be invited as well to participate in such a preparation (see Chapter 3: The Parish).

Gathering

1. Prepare the room by arranging small circles of four or six chairs. The Lectionary, opened to the Fifth Sunday of Lent, is placed, along with an unlighted candle, on a table in a prominent place in the room. The table is draped with a purple cloth.

2. Welcome the participants and allow time for newcomers to be introduced. Invite everyone to be seated in small groups, with the elect and candidates seated with their godparents and sponsors. Begin by stating briefly these or similar words:

   Each week that we celebrate the Rite of Scrutiny, as we have for the past two Sundays during Lent, we are invited deeper and deeper into a great mystery that affects all people. Our world is thirsting, we are thirsting, and Jesus brings us living water. Our world is blind, we are blind, and Jesus opens our eyes. Today we take one step further on our Lenten journey as we open up the Scriptures for the Fifth Sunday of Lent, and our lives in reflection and prayer. Tonight we will name what keeps us, our communities, and our society from life and the true freedom of the children of God. The task for this session is to prepare for the ritual celebration which will take place next Sunday: the last of the three Scrutinies. Part of our preparation is to name what keeps us enmeshed in death and to bring it to prayer.

Prayer

1. Invite everyone to close their eyes and to take several deep breaths, breathing out the tiredness or stresses of the day and breathing in the freshness of God's presence.

2. Sing "Canticle of the Turning" (Rory Cooney, GIA Publications, Inc., 1990).

3. Pray in these or your own words:

   Good and gracious God,
   we gather to reflect on our lives, our communities, and our society,
   and to discern how we are responding to your call to be disciples of your Son, Jesus Christ.
   Send your Spirit to be with us, to strengthen us, and to lead us in this reflection.
   We trust in your promise to be with us always.
   We pray this in the name of Jesus, our brother.
   Amen.

Reflection

1. Invite everyone to listen to a proclamation of the Gospel for the Fifth Sunday of Lent, Year A. Proclaim John 11:1–45 or play the recording of this Gospel by David Haas (*Who Calls You By Name*, Vol. II, GIA Publications, Inc., 1988).

2. After several minutes of silent reflection, Invite the participants to remain in their small groups and reflect on what in our world, both secular and ecclesial, keeps us bound. Allow some time for discussion, then invite the groups to share with the whole group what they discussed. Write the results of their discussion on newsprint, chalkboard, or on an overhead transparency for all to see.

3. Proclaim the end of the Gospel passage, John 11:38–45.

4. After a moment of quiet reflection, comment, using these or similar words:

   Jesus directs them to take away the stone. He then calls out to Lazarus, who does come forth bound in burial cloths. Jesus then commands those present to untie him and let him go free. Lazarus needed the help of others in order to be freed of that which held him bound. Others must help us to become unbound too.

5. Invite participants to discuss in their small groups the ways we need to reach out to others in order to untie them. Ask them to name persons and/or groups that we hold bound and to discuss how it is that we hold such persons/groups bound and the ways we need to untie them.

6. After fifteen to twenty minutes, invite the participants to share with the whole group the names of the people they mentioned and the ways in which we need to untie others. Have someone record their responses again on newsprint, chalkboard, or on an overhead transparency. Tell the participants that what you have written down will be used in the Scrutiny to be celebrated on Sunday.

7. Invite them to spend some time sharing with one other person in their small groups a story of a personal experience of being bound, making sure to name who helped to untie them.

8. After fifteen minutes or so, invite everyone to gather back together into the large group.

Closing

Light the candle and then invite each person to pray either a petition asking God for deliverance from what holds them bound or a prayer of thanksgiving for a time in which they were delivered from bondage. Chant "God of the Living, Not of the Dead" (David Haas, GIA Publications, Inc., 1988), several times.

Chapter 6
Resources for Retreats

Introduction

Two sample retreats are offered in this chapter. One is a full day retreat and the other is an overnight retreat, which includes an evening and a full day. If time is limited, any segment of each of these two retreats may be adapted for use in an evening of reflection or an afternoon retreat. Each segment can stand alone. The themes for reflection are: "Journeys of Conversion," "The Meaning of Baptism," "God Chooses Us," "Opening to God," and "Cost of Discipleship." Within the context of the section Opening to God, the option for celebrating the sacrament of Penance with the baptized candidates is suggested.

The final piece is a prayer experience to be used on Holy Saturday. This sample format can be adapted to accommodate the time available and the needs of your particular group of people.

Full Day Retreat

Setting the Tone
(thirty minutes)

Opening Prayer

Three Journeys of Conversion

Reflection on Personal Journey of Conversion

The Meaning of Baptism

Bearers of the Good News

Closing

Overnight Retreat

Setting the Tone

First Evening: God Chooses Us

Morning: Opening to God

Afternoon: Cost of Discipleship

Setting the Tone

Prior to the retreat: Mail or distribute a letter of invitation to the retreat asking the participants to bring a Bible and a notebook for journaling. Arrange the room with a circle of chairs, and display photographs of the elect and candidates (snapshots of the various events along the journey of the catechumenate). Be sure to duplicate copies of the handouts you will be using. Arrange a centerpiece on the floor in the center of the circle of chairs. Place a large glass bowl of water on a nicely arranged purple cloth, along with a lighted candle. To this basic centerpiece you may add flowers and other symbols that tell the story of the journey of the elect and candidates in your parish.

Day of the retreat: Greet each participant upon arrival. Have coffee, muffins, and fruit available and allow about thirty minutes for visiting and refreshments.

Opening Prayer

Gather the group by playing a recording of some instrumental music and inviting the participants to take a place in the circle of chairs. You might use one of the many recordings which offer sounds of water.

When all have been seated, begin the prayer in these or similar words of your own:

> *Wind upon the waters, voice whispering in the wind and sea.*
> *You are the Word of God.*
> *You are the Wisdom of God.*
> *Bubble up in us as waters from the depth of the earth.*
> *Speak your living Word and Wisdom to each of us this day.*
> *Your Word is Truth and Light,*
> *Your Wisdom blazes like a flame, cutting through pretense, fear, and evil.*
> *Redeem us from the patterns which cause destruction in our lives.*
> *Create in us newness, energy for life, and a passion for justice.*

> *Bless our time together this day*
> *as we prepare to enter into the fullness of your life with this community of faith.*
> *We ask you to hear our prayer in the name of Jesus. Amen.*

Three Journeys of Conversion

1. Recall with the group a sense of the Lenten season. Use the information from Chapter 1 of this manual to compose a very short presentation that includes these points:

   - Lent is a sacred journey into the death and resurrection of Christ. During this journey, we focus on our own conversion through prayer, fasting, and almsgiving. The community of the faithful stands with the elect as they make their final preparations for the Sacraments of Initiation.

   - This time of purification and enlightenment involves a balance between the penitential nature of this season and the reclaiming of God's call to us to prepare for baptism or for the renewal of our baptism.

2. Invite the participants to listen to the Word of God, saying this:

   > *The three journeys of faith we are about to hear proclaimed are reminders of the faith journey we have experienced these past several months. As you hear these Scripture passages proclaimed, listen and discern your own experience of growth.*

   A. Journey of Covenant:

   Invite a sponsor to proclaim Genesis 12:1–5, 17:1–8.

   After a moment of silent reflection, explain that this covenant promise made to Abraham is our promise too. Invite the elect and candidates to share their *initial* reactions to this passage with their godparents and sponsors. Then invite them to discuss these questions:

- What hopes have been fulfilled in you as you journeyed in faith these months?

- How has God's promised presence been part of your journey?

B. Journey to Freedom:

Ask a team member to proclaim Exodus 14:15–15:1.

After a moment of silent reflection, point out that the journey of the Israelites from slavery to freedom is a universal story of God's desire to free us of all that holds us captive. Encourage the participants to continue sharing their insights into this passage in the same groups. After a brief discussion time, offer these questions for further discussion:

- On your journey toward freedom thus far, how has God set you free?

- What signs of God's healing, liberation, and forgiveness have you experienced?

C. Journey of Jesus:

Ask one of the godparents to proclaim Luke 19:41–47, the journey of Jesus.

After a moment of silent reflection, explain that Jesus' journey to Jerusalem was a journey to the cross because he stood for the marginalized and against the entrenched and established powers of evil. Invite the small groups to react to the Scriptures and to follow their initial discussion by sharing responses to these questions:

- What has taking up the cross meant in your journey of conversion?

- What experiences of working for justice have enriched your time of preparation?

Have everyone take a fifteen minute break. Serve light refreshments such as coffee and juice.

Reflection on Personal Journey of Conversion

1. Gather the participants back into the circle. Invite them to relax, and prepare them to pray in silence. Help them look back on their journey of conversion using this centering prayer.

   Allow yourself to become silent, becoming aware of your heartbeat and your breathing. Imagine you are in a beautiful meadow. It is your favorite season—what time of year is it? Imagine the insect sounds . . . the birds . . . the scent of flowers, leaves, and grass.

   You find yourself seated on a warm round rock, next to a flowing stream. You relax and become mesmerized by the flowing water. You watch the reflections of the flowers, the grass, the sky in the stream . . . soon you find yourself totally soothed by the running water and the reflections passing before your eyes.

   You notice the reflections take on a new look. You begin to see scenes . . . people . . . places . . . that look familiar. You notice that these are people and places from your past. Your life flows by in the swirling waters. You are a young child—your first memory flashes in the water. Are you happy or crying, . . . warmly held close to your mother, . . . or alone in your crib? God's love whirls through you at this time in your life, weaving its path of warmth and abundance.

   You now see yourself as a child in school. Are you confident or afraid, . . . comfortable or insecure, . . . happy or sad? Again, as the water flows over the scene of your childhood, you are aware of God soothing your sadness and pain and loving you just as you are.

   The scene shifts to your adolescent years. What was this time of your life like for you? What were your feelings? What were your experiences? As you look back, be assured that God quenches all your thirsts and satisfies all your longings.

Come now to the present time of your life. What crises and difficulties have you experienced these past months? What joys and moments of peace have accompanied you on your journey of conversion? Who has loved you? In what relationship do you seek peace? God is ever present, like the soft wind blowing across the meadow—like the eddies of the rolling stream. God loves all of you without condition, without your deserving it. God finds you irresistible!

Slowly and gently return to this place. Take up your pen and journal and begin to write. Write whatever comes to mind from this meditation. Write about your lifetime journey of conversion.

Allow enough time for the group to reflect and write in silence.

2. When they have finished writing in their journals, direct everyone to spend about thirty minutes alone and reflect specifically upon their most recent journey toward full initiation into the Catholic community. Encourage them to note in their journals important turning points along that journey. A good question with which to send them off alone might be: How have you walked the journey of covenant, freedom, and the cross as you prepare for the Sacraments of Initiation?

3. Signal the group as the end of the reflection time nears. Then after a few minutes, invite the participants to return to their small groups: Have them share responses to these questions:

> What do you fear or what other emotions or challenges does this final step on the journey evoke in you?

For those preparing for baptism or renewing their baptism:

> What must die in you that you can rise to new life?

The Meaning of Baptism

1. Invite a member of the team to read Matthew 3:13–17, the account of Jesus' baptism. Present a comparison between Jesus' baptism and our baptism. Take care to make the distinction between affirming the baptism of the candidates and the future baptism of the elect. This outline will offer some help in preparing your presentation:

A. Jesus' Baptism and Our Baptism

1. A voice spoke, "This is my beloved son" (3:17, NAB).

2. We have been made friends of God through the saving action of Jesus.

   a. Chosen and named as God's own

   b. Held in the palm of God's hands as claimed by the psalmist

   c. Empowered for mission by the sacrament of Baptism

B. Jesus' Temptation and Our Forty Days of Lent

1. (For Jesus, his experience in the desert is a preparation for mission. For us, these forty days of Lent, of purification and enlightenment, have been our preparation.)

2. Jesus came . . .

   a. to bring good news to the poor . . .

   b. to heal the blind . . .

   c. to liberate the imprisoned . . .

   d. to announce God's favor.

3. Our baptismal mission is the same as Jesus' mission.

2. Invite the participants to discuss the mission of the baptized as it flows from the mission of Jesus. Begin in small groups the discussion by asking: How are we called to do what Jesus did in his ministry as revealed in the Gospel? When participants finish discussing responses, have them take a stretch break before beginning the last segment of the retreat.

Bearers of the Good News

1. Prior to this last segment of the retreat, select two team members to speak the roles of the woman at the well and Cleopas, who was one of the people who met Jesus on the road to Emmaus.

2. After the brief stretch break, invite the participants to return to their small groups. Briefly explain that two readers will present a dramatic dialogue between the woman at the well and Cleopas, one of the people who met Jesus on the road to Emmaus. Encourage them to enter into the story to discover the next steps in the never-ending journey of conversion and to open their hearts and ears to hear the story of these messengers of the Good News.

3. The readers may begin, using this script:

Reader One: *I am a woman, so often looked down upon in this male-controlled world. Furthermore, I am the wrong religion, despised by the Jews, considered unclean, just because I have many gods to worship.*

Reader Two: *We are two young men. I am Cleopas, my companion is nameless—perhaps it is you. We are too young and uneducated to understand all the events of these last days. Confused and upset, we are ignored. It's easy to get overlooked in the illustrious circles of rabbis, scribes, and other religious leaders.*

Reader One: *He spoke to me at a well . . . the well, a sign of life. Water in this desert place is precious. Wells are places where the ancient ones met their marriage partners, Jacob and Rachel . . . Rebecca and Isaac. This is a well outside the city of Jerusalem, about as far from the Jewish center as you could get.*

Reader Two: *He spoke to us on the road. . . . a stranger joined in step with us on that dusty highway to Emmaus . . . a well-traveled road . . . a road away from Jerusalem. In fright, we took flight from that center of our faith.*

Reader One: *He spoke of thirst and waters. This rabbi . . . who once took pity on a bridegroom at a wedding in Cana when they ran out of wine . . . He spoke to me of his thirst, my thirst. Cana . . . the best of all wine for last. He promised and spoke of never thirsting again.*

Reader Two: *He spoke of the prophets of old, explaining with patience the heritage of hope given to a nation, a chosen people. He was tolerant without youthful babbling and confusion. He looked at us with kindness and spoke with wisdom.*

Reader One: *He spoke to me, a woman, nameless, but the symbol of all of Samaria. He told me of my many idols, spoke of the break of my tribe with the one true God, our worship of Baal, and the sin of my people. Like a bridegroom he attracted me.*

Reader Two: *Fascinated with the authority and clarity of his interpretation . . . a fire started in our hearts. Excitement overcame us! Never had we heard the Scriptures explained so profoundly!*

Reader One: *I was overcome with joy! I had to call my people . . . those who wait for Moses' return. I had to share my experience of living waters . . . of life so abundant . . . of all the secrets and narrowness of our tribe. I felt as though I would burst wide open with the wisdom and understanding of this teacher.*

Reader Two: *He made as if to go on and leave us. We could not let this happen. We wanted so much more, so we invited him to dine with us. Then as he broke bread, we recognized him clearly. We knew in that instant that Jesus, the Messiah, had risen as the women had said.*

Reader One: *I called them together and said, "Come and see this teacher I met at the well! Could this be the Messiah? The one we have waited for?" They were charged with my excitement and followed me to see for themselves. He stayed with us for several days. I, the name-less woman, the unclean Samaritan, was compelled to share my joyful good news. I was his disciple, his herald of the largesse of the Kingdom of God!*

Reader Two: *With all the impetuousness of youth, we rushed back to Jerusalem to tell all the followers that truly he had risen. We— young, frightened, confused by the events of these past days— had a new clarity about our mission to tell our story to all who would listen . . . we are never too young to be bearers of the Good News!*

4. Invite everyone to spend a few moments to reflect privately on the dialogue. Then ask participants to share with the members of their small groups their insights gained from hearing and reflecting on the parallel presentation.

5. Ask everyone to gather as a large group. Invite participants to name how they are called to be disciples: bearers of the Good News.

Closing

Close the retreat by asking all to stand and pray the Lord's Prayer. (If the Lord's Prayer has not yet been presented, close instead by singing "We Are Called" [David Haas, GIA Publications, Inc., 1988] or some other appropriate hymn on the theme of sharing the Good News.)

Setting the Tone

Arrange to have the retreat at a site away from the parish that has overnight accommodations for all the participants. A nearby retreat house or convent will work well. Send a formal invitation to the elect, the candidates, sponsors, godparents, and team members.

Prior to the retreat, arrange a room with a circle of chairs. In the center of the circle place a purple cloth, a large flat bowl of sand, a cross, and some desert plants, such as cacti. Use other appropriate art objects and natural elements to create a desert-like environment. Have a small taper on each chair for the participants or distribute the tapers when all gather for prayer.

Greet each participant upon arrival. Provide some light refreshment, snacks, or beverages for the group as a sign of hospitality. Allow about one-half hour for registration, room assignments, unpacking, and visiting.

First Evening: God Chooses Us

Opening Prayer

1. Gather the group. Invite them to bring their chairs into a circle and have them be seated. Explain the general theme of the retreat is "entering the desert." Invite volunteers to name some of the symbols in the room that offer a feel for the desert. Briefly ask them to share what words or phrases they associate with the "desert" or with a "retreat."

2. Ask the participants, one by one, to name their hopes for this retreat. After each participant names their hopes, direct them to light a taper and place it in the sand in the large flat bowl.

3. When all have had a chance to share their hopes for the retreat, invite them to prayer. Begin by asking all to stand and sing "I Have Loved You" (Michael Joncas, New Dawn Music, 1979) or a similar hymn. Invite everyone to be seated for the meditation.

4. Proclaim Isaiah 43:1–4. Pause for a few moments, allowing all to reflect on the Word of God that has just been proclaimed.

Meditation on God's Chosen

1. Prior to the prayer invite two team members to prepare to prayerfully proclaim the adaptation of Isaiah 43:1–4. Instruct them to read slowly and deliberately and to alternate parts as indicated below.

2. Explain to the participants that the following meditation is based upon the passage they just heard proclaimed from the prophet Isaiah. Invite them to close their eyes and listen as God speaks these words directly to them.

First Reader: *But now, thus says the Lord,*
who created you, O Jacob,
and formed you, O Israel.
*I, **the Lord**, have created you.*
I who formed the earth,
the oceans and the land, the
sun and the stars, and
millions and
millions of people, created YOU.
*I **created** you.*
I brought you out of nothing-
ness into life.
I breathed the very breath of
life into you.
I created you. I created YOU.
I made you, you.
I wanted YOU to be part of my
creation.
I wanted YOU:
  To be alive
  To be who you are,
  With your talents and gifts,
  With your hair and eyes
  and facial features;
  With your hands and
  body, and within your
  family.
I, the Lord of Life . . . created
you. (Pause.)

Second Reader: *I have formed you, O Israel. I have been forming you from your very first moments of life. I have been watching over you—caring for you . . . providing for you . . .*

keeping my hand ever beside you— each and every day of your life. I formed you through the early years of your childhood. I watched you begin school . . . run and play. I formed you as you began getting a little older, making your own decisions. I formed you through your struggles and joys, hopes, and dreams. I have been forming you in your journey that led you here—to this place—at this time. I have been with you in your questions and insights. I have truly formed you. (Pause.)

First Reader: *Fear not, for I have redeemed you; I have called you by name; you are mine. Do not be afraid, for I am always with you. I know your name—it is written in the palm of my hand. I knew you even from the time you were formed in your mother's womb. I know what you think and feel. I know you—and you know me. You are mine. Your heart and your spirit will always find rest in me—for you are mine. (Pause.)*

Second Reader: *When you pass through the waters, I will be with you; In the rivers you shall not drown. When you walk through fire— you shall not be burned; The flames shall not consume you. There is nothing to fear—not even floods and fire; I will always take care of you. There is nothing to fear—not the future—not any problem; I will always take care of you. Whatever you are afraid of, come to me, and I will take care of you. (Pause.)*

First Reader: *For I am the Lord, your God, the Holy One of Israel, your Savior. I, the Lord, your God am Holy. I am full of love and goodness. No matter how great you imagine my love to be, it is always greater. I love without end or limit or reason. For I am God. (Pause.)*

Second Reader: *I give Egypt as your ransom, Ethiopia and Sheba in return for you. You are worth everything to me. You are so valued. Why? Simply because you are precious in my eyes and because I love you. I see how glorious you truly are; I see the goodness in your heart and all that you give to others; I see your hopes and your dreams and your love.*

You are precious—you are really invaluable to me.
What does it mean to you if someone is precious?
You prize them and gently hold them.
*I say to you, you are **precious** in my eyes.* (Pause.)

First Reader: *Because I love you*
I want you to know how much I love you,
I love you as you are.
You don't have to be different: heavier or thinner, taller or shorter, or more patient or less angry.
I LOVE YOU!
I love you because I under-stand you—your hurts, your struggles, your concerns, and your motives.
I know your hopes and dreams.
I love you.
Never forget this.
I LOVE YOU!

Invite everyone to remain, for the next ten minutes, in the presence of the God who made and formed each one of us.

3. After the participants have reflected on the meditation, ask them to write their feelings and reactions to the meditation in their journals. Allow an additional ten minutes.

4. Gather the participants into small groups consisting of two elect or candidates and two godparents or sponsors. Ask them to spend some time discussing these questions:

   • What were your reactions and feelings during the reflection on God's love from the Book of the Prophet Isaiah?

   • What will it take for you to accept this unconditional love?

   • How do you hope to respond to God's love?

5. After allowing sufficient time for sharing, ask all to stand and sing "Here I Am, Lord" (Dan Schutte, New Dawn Music, 1981). Close the mediation by praying in these or similar words:

   God of creation,
   you have called us into the desert of Lent and into this retreat.
   We rejoice that we have come!
   You have offered us your unconditional love from the moment of our creation in your divine image.
   You have reminded us that we were formed and valued by you even from the time when we were in our mother's womb.
   You have promised to be with us everywhere and always.
   God of the Promise, we know that we were chosen by you to be what we are.
   Bless us as we sleep in the knowledge of your loving embrace.
   Through Jesus in the power of the Holy Spirit, we pray. Amen.

Morning: Opening to God

Opening Prayer

1. Before this morning session, invite a team member to lead the prayer, and one of the god-parents or sponsors to proclaim the Scriptures. Allow enough time for them to prepare.

2. After breakfast begin the morning by greeting any new arrivals. Then proceed with this prayer service or one that you have created.

Gathering

Greeting: *Last evening we spent time with God's great love for us. It is in the light of that love that we can see places within ourselves that are not yet fully open to the Lord. This morning we gather with the sense that God is calling each of us to open ourselves even more to our fullest possibilities. Let us begin our prayer with a few moments of silent reflection to discover God's presence here with us today and to listen to God's invitation.*

Gathering Hymn: All stand and sing "Canticle of the Sun" (Marty Haugen, GIA Publications, Inc., 1980).

Gathering Prayer:

> *God of Love, we are your people.*
> *You have created and formed us from the very beginning.*
> *You gather us together as your beloved sons and daughters.*
> *Open our hearts, minds, and souls to hear your Word. Crack open the shell of fear so that we might receive all that you desire for us.*
> *We are yours and you are our God, now and forever. Amen.*

Proclamation of the Word of God

Reading: All sit as a godparent or sponsor proclaims the Scriptures. Ezekiel 36:24–28.

Silent Reflection: All silently reflect on what God has spoken to them.

Intercessions: The presider, or leader, invites all to stand. The presider leads the intercessions, then invites members of the group to pray their own intercessions.

Closing Hymn: All sing "You Are the Voice," (David Haas, GIA Publications, Inc., 1983). All sit after the hymn is sung.

Extended Reflection or Optional Celebration of the Sacrament of Penance

1. Before you begin the reflection, share some thoughts with the group on the theme "Opening to God." Make sure to cover these points:

   - Just as a flower opens to the sun, we are called to open our whole being to God.

   This means that our body, soul, mind, and imagination—indeed, our whole self—are vulnerable before God.

   - God knows the secrets of our hearts. When we can name our shortcomings, our failures, and our sins, it is not to let God in on our hidden selves, but it is more that we open our weaknesses to the light of God's love. In that light, all can be forgiven, healed, and set free.

   - To be vulnerable takes much trust. Do we trust God enough to be this open? Jesus came to reassure us that God is abundantly merciful. God is the unconditional loving Parent, who is ready to embrace us even before we have a chance to ask for forgiveness. God will not quench a faltering wick or stomp on a bruised reed. Look at the love and acceptance of sinners in the stories of Jesus' encounters in the Gospels.

   - Are you ready to turn your whole self over to God? Can you feel the comfort of his loving gaze as you speak to God of even your deepest secrets? Are you ready to let God be the Lord of your life?

2. Invite the participants to go off alone to reflect upon those areas of their life that they need to open up before God and bring to the light. Distribute a copy of a simple examination of conscience (See Handout of reflection questions on pages 163–164.) to each participant as they spend time alone. Encourage them to write in their journals.

   This would also be a good time to offer an opportunity for the baptized to celebrate the sacrament of Penance. If you choose this option, distribute copies of the handout on the sacrament of Reconciliation, page 161.

3. After about an hour of sacred time alone, invite the elect and candidates to pair up with their godparents and sponsors to share the insights gleaned from this time of prayer and interior opening to God. In their discussion ask the pairs to share:

- Concrete ways they have opened themselves to God as they have walked this spiritual journey of conversion over the past several months.

- Areas in their life where they still feel that they are holding out, that is, those barriers in their life where they do not yet respond fully and freely to the call of God.

Invite the godparents and sponsors, with the input of the elect or candidates, to create a petition that reflects the barriers named by the elect or candidates. Have them begin each petition with "Loving God, I bring to you my . . . I ask you to bless me with . . . that I might be more open."

Explain that these petitions will be part of petition in prayer concluding the morning session. When the participants have finished writing, ask them to place these intercessions in a bowl provided in the center of the circle.

Closing Prayer

Leader: Invite everyone to stand.

Assembly: All stand and sing "Change Our Hearts," (Rory Cooney, North American Liturgy Resources, 1984).

Leader: God of all mercy, you have come to set us free from guilt and shame. Lord have mercy.

All: Lord, have mercy.

Leader: God of goodness and grace, you have filled us to overflowing with your blessings and love. Christ have mercy.

All: Christ, have mercy.

Leader: God of justice and peace, you are present with us always, guiding us in the ways of harmony and nonviolence. Lord have mercy.

All: Lord, have mercy.

Proclamation of the Word of God

Reader: Proclaim Ezekiel 38:24–28.

Assembly: Sit and silently reflect on first reading.

Reader: Invite all to stand and proclaim Luke 15:11–32. Then invite all to sit and reflect on the Gospel, asking this question: What does Jesus reveal about God's mercy in this parable?

Leader: Read the intercessions one at a time.

Assembly: All sing "Lord, change our hearts" after each petition.

Leader: Invite all to stand and sing the concluding hymn.

Assembly: Sing "Lift Up Your Hearts" (Roc O'Connor, S.J., New Dawn Music, 1981).

Optional: As an alternative to the closing prayer service, you may wish to celebrate at this time the Presentation of the Lord's Prayer (RCIA, 180–182), using the readings suggested in the ritual text.

Afternoon: Cost of Discipleship

1. Having agreed prior to the gathering, ask two godparents and sponsors to offer a witness of discipleship based upon Matthew 5:1–16.

2. After everyone has gathered, open the afternoon session. Invite all to listen and hear as you proclaim Matthew 5:1–16. Let the group sit for a few moments of silence after the Word is proclaimed.

3. Invite the godparents and sponsors who have agreed to give witness, to give their witness talks.

4. Have the group gather into smaller groups and share their initial reactions to the Gospel and the witness talks. Ask them to discuss:

   - What did you hear that was startling or challenging?

   - What words gave you comfort?

Then ask each small group to determine one thing that God wants of us as disciples.

5. Invite the small groups to share with the large group the quality of a disciple they named. On several large sheets of newsprint have someone record the responses so that everyone can read them.

6. Invite all to silently reflect on the list of qualities identifying what it means to be a disciple. After a few minutes of reflection, distribute paper and envelopes. Then instruct the participants to write a letter to themselves naming what their commitment to be a follower of Jesus means to them. Encourage them to be specific and concrete, particularly regarding their call to share the Good News and bear justice and peace to all. When they have had sufficient time to write, ask each person to seal the letter in an envelope and address it to him- or herself. Explain that these letters will be mailed back to each person in one year as a reminder of the retreat, their conversion journey, and their commitment. (You may wish to plan a time of recommitment one year from now at a retreat for the newly initiated. At that time they can examine their past year in the light of their call to discipleship.)

Gather the participants into pairs for the closing prayer—the elect with godparents and candidates with sponsors. Ask them to share one thing they have taken to heart regarding their call to discipleship. Then invite the participants to gather in the circle as "disciples," personally called by Jesus to be his followers with a mission to the world. Continue with this prayer or one that you develop to suit your group.

Gathering

Assembly: All sing the hymn "Blest Are They" (David Haas, GIA Publications, Inc., 1985).

Gathering Prayer:

Lead everyone in praying the gathering prayer:

Leader: *We give thanks, Yahweh!*
Our gathering this day has renewed and refreshed us.
Filled with hope, we leave this place, to carry your love to all we meet.
Our praise of your name is on our lips.

Assembly: *Our hearts are grateful to you, Yahweh, whose name resounds throughout the universe.*

Proclamation of the Word of God

Reader: Proclaim Matthew 25:31–46.

Assembly: Reflect upon the call to discipleship in the light of this Word of God, as soft instrumental music plays in the background.

Leader: Invite the godparents and sponsors to place their hands on the shoulders or head of the elect or candidates and pray in silence for them as they commit themselves to following Jesus.

Prayer of Thanksgiving

(Distribute copies of the handout on page 165.)

Leader: *We give thanks, Yahweh. We have shared our stories—stories of lives filled with your constant care and presence. As we face the mission of carrying your Good News to all people, remove our fears and inspire us with the energetic fire of the Holy Spirit that your Word may inspire generations to come.*

Assembly: *Our hearts are grateful to you, Yahweh, whose name resounds throughout the universe.*

Leader: *We give thanks, Yahweh! Your compassion for us has led us to care for one another and to commit ourselves to work together in serving the needs of others. Teach us to serve without arrogance or the need for recognition, to heal with humility and a gentle touch, and to offer help with a heart open to receive the help of others. Fill us with love and empower us to reconcile your people and your world that your presence in us might transform our communities, country, and world.*

Assembly: *Our hearts are grateful to you, Yahweh, whose name resounds throughout the universe.*

Leader: *We give thanks, Yahweh! The Good News, made real in the person of Jesus, reveals to us, more clearly, who you are. You sent your Word to dwell with us that our words might reach our brothers and sisters in every nation, culture, and society with the Gospel. Let your Word not be spoken in vain. Let your Word yield a rich harvest. Let your Word accomplish all you have begun in our hearts this day.*

Assembly: *Our hearts are grateful to you, Yahweh, whose name resounds throughout the universe.*

Leader: *We give thanks, Yahweh! As we discover, once again, the power of the Paschal Mystery—the dying and rising of Jesus—we pray that the power of the eucharistic table will continually renew, refresh, and empower us with a fervor for Jesus' mission, bringing Good News to the poor, the imprisoned, the blind, the marginalized, and the unclean. May all be welcomed at your table and in our hearts and communities so that when we join you at the banquet of heaven, we might also be welcomed.*

Assembly: *Our hearts are grateful to you, Yahweh, whose Name resounds throughout the universe.*

Leader: *We give thanks, Yahweh! Today, we have discovered anew the presence and power of your Spirit. Your Spirit has preserved us as a People of God throughout history. Your Spirit has inspired prophets and preachers, setting a fire on this earth. Your Spirit has led us through the dark night of tragedy and crises, opening us even more to receive your love. We pray that this Holy Spirit will give us the courage to speak truth, purify us of all prejudice, strengthen us when we are weak and weary, and grace us with joy as we walk the journey of our call to discipleship.*

Assembly: *Our hearts are grateful to you, Yahweh, whose name resounds throughout the universe.*

Closing Hymn

Assembly: Sing "We are Called" (David Haas, GIA Publications, Inc., 1988).

Preparing the Space

Prior to the gathering, arrange the room with chairs for the elect and candidates, the sponsors and godparents in a circle around a centerpiece that has been decorated with symbols for Holy Saturday. You may wish to include a large rock to represent the sealed tomb, a white cloth to symbolize the burial cloth of Jesus, a cross as a sign of discipleship, or any appropriate symbol that helps your group. Enthrone the Bible on an ambo or on a table in the center of the circle.

Opening Prayer: Gathered in God's Presence

1. Call the group to the circle of chairs. Begin the prayer by inviting the elect and candidates to name and share with the group their desires as they approach the sacraments of Initiation. After the elect and candidates have finished, invite the godparents and the sponsors or the team to share any reflections they have.

2. Pray in these or your own words:

   We come together in your presence, O God.
   You have created us out of love.
   You have redeemed us through the life,
   *   death, and resurrection of your Son, Jesus*
   *   Christ.*
   You call us to unity with one another and
   *   into your mission*
   for the sake of the world
   under the guidance and energy of the Holy
   *   Spirit.*
   Be with us now during this time of prayer.
   Amen.

   Invite all to stand and sing verses 1 and 2 of "Now We Remain" (David Haas, GIA Publications, Inc., 1983).

Proclamation of the Word: Drawing from the Waters of Salvation

1. After a short time of silence, continue by praying this:

   Let us pray.
   Yahweh, faithful God, we will receive your
   *   Son, Jesus, in the form of bread and wine*
   *   this evening.*
   Open us that we might be willing to be your
   *   bread for the world.*
   Enlarge our hearts that we might be willing
   *   to be broken and shared for the life of*
   *   others.*
   Enlighten our minds and hearts, our entire
   *   being to you and your life.*
   We pray this in the name of Jesus Christ.
   Amen.

2. Invite a team member to proclaim Isaiah 12:2–6. After a moment of quiet reflection, ask the participants to share their responses to this reading in pairs. When they have finished, invite several volunteers to share the insights they gleaned from the reflection and sharing in the large group.

3. Optional: If the Creed was presented to the elect (and candidates) earlier in Lent, introduce the Recitation of the Creed now by saying:

   We will all draw water at the fountain of
   salvation tonight. Some of us will enter the
   waters of baptism for the first time. The rest—
   candidates, sponsors, and the entire
   community—will come to the waters of
   baptism to be renewed and refreshed. To
   prepare for this encounter with the waters of
   salvation, we will make our baptismal
   promises either for the first time or we will
   renew the promises made at our baptism. We
   will be asked, "Do you believe?" Do you
   believe? Some weeks ago the Church
   entrusted to the elect (and candidates) this
   precious symbol of faith, the Creed. At that
   time you listened to us as we said to you "I
   believe." We hope that the words we spoke at

that time have echoed in your hearts. Now it is time for us to listen to you as you say "I believe" in preparation for that moment when you will profess your faith before the whole Church tonight.

The elect and candidates recite the Creed. If the Creed was not presented earlier, omit this section and move directly to number 4.

4. Invite all to join in singing "You Shall Be My People," (Michael Ward, World Library Publications, 1989) or "Jesus Christ, Yesterday, Today and for Ever" (Suzanne Toolan, GIA Publications, Inc., 1988) or some other appropriate hymn.

Closing: Come to the Lord

1. Recall with the elect and candidates the Rite of Acceptance when they expressed before the community of the faithful what they sought from God and the community. Invite them, as they approach the sacraments of Initiation, to share with their godparents and sponsors what they now ask of God and God's Church. Encourage them to reflect silently before they begin sharing, by looking deeply within themselves to find their heart's longing. During this longer period of sharing, play a recording of some instrumental flute background music.

2. When they have finished sharing, bring their attention back to the large group by playing a recording of or singing two verses of "Come To the Water" (John Foley, New Dawn Music, 1978). Invite everyone to look back on their journey of conversion, their journey of initiation, and to discover the blessings God has bestowed upon them. Continue playing "Come to the Water" very softly in the background.

When everyone has had a few moments to recall their blessings, invite them to share with the large group one blessing for which they are grateful. After each person shares a blessing, pray the response, *God of life, we thank you.*

3. Invite the elect and candidates to stand, forming a circle in the center of the room. Ask the godparents and sponsors to surround and enclose them by placing their hands on the elect and candidates and praying:

*Loving and faithful God,
keep [individual names of the elect or candidates are spoken aloud] ever close to you.
Protect them from all evil.
Remove anything that holds them back from surrendering totally into your loving embrace
Open them and heal them with your love.
Strengthen and sustain them to go forth from these sacraments of Initiation to be your disciples to a world that needs them.
May we always remain faithful to you
and to the unity you have created among your people and all of your creation. May Jesus Christ be the Lord of all our lives, now and forever. Amen.*

Ask everyone to sing "Amazing Grace."

Appendix
HANDOUTS

Reflection

1. To hear my name called made me feel . . .

2. To hear testimony given on my behalf was . . .

3. For me to be called forth and to sign the Book of the Elect meant . . .

4. As a candidate, I understand that by my baptism my name is already in the Book of Elect, which makes me feel . . .

Discussion

For discussion between elect and godparents and candidates and sponsors:

Who are you named after?

Who do you know and admire that has the same name?

What do you know about saints who bear the same name as yours or a derivative thereof?

What does it mean to be called by name by God? By this community?

What is your response to such a call?

Reflection

1. When I heard testimony given on my behalf I felt (thought) . . .

2. When I heard my name called to come forth and sign the Book of the Elect I was . . .

3. For me to sign the Book of the Elect means . . .

4. As a candidate, to know that my name is already entered into the Book of the Elect means to me that . . .

5. I understand my election by God voiced by the Church means . . .

Discussion

For discussion between elect and godparents and candidates and sponsors:

1. For me, I experience the desert or wilderness as . . .

2. The direction my life is going right now is . . .

3. The struggles I experience in striving to live a Christian life are . . .

4. I want to deepen my relationship with God by . . .

5. I want to deepen my commitment to be an active member of this community by . . .

Reflection

1. For me the experience of hearing my name called was like . . .

2. The word or phrase which I want to remember from this Rite is . . .

3. To sign the Book of the Elect meant to me . . .

4. To hear others testify on my behalf made me feel like . . .

5. To know that by my Baptism I am already a member of God's elect made me feel (realize) . . .

Discussion

For discussion between elect and godparents and candidates and sponsors:

1. My relationship with God is . . .

   What I can do to strengthen my relationship with God is . . .

2. My relationship with other people is . . .

   What I can do to improve my relationship with other people is . . .

   The works of charity which would help to put me in a right relationship with others are . . .

3. My relationship with things is . . .

   What I can do to have a better balance in my relationship with things is . . .

   The type of fasting that would help me to have more harmony (balance) in my life would be . . .

Reflection

1. Images I heard or experienced in the Liturgy of the Word were . . .

2. These images confirm my understanding of discipleship as . . .

3. To me the mountain and the conversation with Jesus, Moses, and Elijah symbolizes . . .

(IF PENITENTIAL RITE IS CELEBRATED)

1. During this Rite I felt . . .

2. In this Rite I heard . . .

3. In this Rite I was affirmed in and challenged to . . .

Discussion

For discussion between elect and godparents and candidates and sponsors:

1. I spoke to Jesus about . . .

2. Jesus spoke to me about . . .

3. Someone or something that helped me to recall that God invited me to walk this journey was . . .

4. I continue to hear God's choice of me and I respond by . . .

5. I try to deepen my relationship with God and my neighbor by . . .

My prayer is . . .

Reflection

1. In this liturgy I heard (experienced) . . .

2. To me the Transfiguration is . . .

3. My relationship with Jesus is . . .

(IF THE PENITENTIAL RITE IS CELEBRATED)

1. During this Rite I felt . . .

2. In this Rite I heard . . .

3. In this Rite I was affirmed in and challenged to . . .

Discussion

For discussion between elect and godparents and candidates and sponsors:

1. Reflect on your experience of this initiation process. In light of your experience, name ways you have been transfigured or transformed.

2. Reflect and name what remains to be transformed.

3. Just as Peter, James, and John saw a new dimension of Jesus revealed, what new aspects of Jesus are being revealed to you? In what ways are these revelations occurring?

4. The voice told the disciples that Jesus is God's son, the Chosen One, and that they were to listen to him. What does Jesus say to you? What do you need or desire?

My prayer is . . .

Reflection

1. Words and/or phrases which touched me today were . . .

2. In the liturgy today, I experienced . . .

3. The message of today's liturgy is . . .

(IF THE PENITENTIAL RITE IS CELEBRATED)

1. During this Rite I felt . . .

2. In this Rite I heard . . .

3. In this Rite I was affirmed in and challenged to . . .

Discussion

For discussion between elect and godparents and candidates and sponsors:

1. What did the words, phrases, and images of today's liturgy say about discipleship?

2. Baptism clothes one in a dazzling white robe. In what ways do I experience the dying and rising to new life in Jesus Christ?

3. The ways I experience the joys of discipleship are . . .

4. I know and experience the glory of Christ by . . .

My prayer is . . .

Reflection

1. In this Scrutiny what touched me the most or what spoke to me was . . .

2. This Scrutiny Rite proclaims that God is . . .

   that Jesus is . . .

   that grace is . . .

3. The experience of hearing our struggles prayed in the midst of the community was . . .

Discussion

For discussion between elect and godparents and candidates and sponsors:

1. The woman was freed and told the townspeople, "Come and see someone who told me everything I ever did." What parts of yourself that were hidden, not even admitted to you, have you now been freed to name for yourself and to God/Jesus?

2. The woman said, "Sir, you don't have a bucket." After she was freed, she put down her water as she realized Jesus did not need a bucket because he is living water. What are the things you hold on to, such as attitudes or fears, rather than receiving Jesus, who is living water? What ways or things do you need to let go in order to accept the living water which Jesus offers you?

3. How is Jesus living water for you? What are some means you have found helpful to find this living water who is Jesus?

My prayer is . . .

In our empty lives, thirsty for . . . fill us with the living water of . . .
OR
For the courage to change . . . so that we may draw water from the deep well of your compassion and bring that water to a world parched by . . .

Reflection

1. Today's liturgy spoke to me—touched me—this way . . .

2. My ways which are not God's ways are . . .

3. The word or phrase from today's liturgy that I want to ponder this week is . . .

Discussion

For discussion between candidates and sponsors:

1. In what ways are the Ten Commandments foundational to living the Christian life?

2. The commandment I find easiest to keep is . . . for these reasons . . .

3. The commandment I find most difficult to keep is . . . for these reasons . . .

4. The commandments guide our relationship with God and with one another by . . .

My prayer is . .

Reflection

1. Words, phrases, and feelings I experienced in today's liturgy are . . .

2. What the psalm refrain "The Lord is kind and merciful" says to me is . . .

3. The verse I would write for this psalm is . . .

Discussion

For discussion between candidates and sponsors:

1. Contemplate what in your life is in need of repentance or reform.

2. What keeps me from fully embracing the covenant and the call to discipleship that baptism establishes is . . .

3. What keeps me from accepting God's loving mercy is . . .

4. I would need to change . . .

My prayer is . . .

Reflection

1. Several things from this Scrutiny which stood out for me or touched me the most are . . .

2. In response to this Scrutiny Rite in what way(s) I am being drawn into a deeper relationship with God, with Jesus . . .

3. The experience of hearing our struggles prayed in the midst of the community was . . .

Discussion

For discussion between elect and godparents and candidates and sponsors:

1. What is the new sight or vision Jesus is offering you? Is there a part of you—some excuse, belief, feeling, or rationalization—that resists?

2. How are your eyes being opened to see in a new way who Jesus is for you?

3. What is the message of the closing dialogue between Jesus and the Pharisees concerning seeing, blindness, and sin? What are the implications of this dialogue for us, who call ourselves believers?

My prayer is . . .

Lord Jesus, I bring you my blindness of . . . Heal me, and give me your true sight.

Reflection

1. Today's liturgy spoke to me or touched me in this way . . .

2. The way(s) I experience God's abounding love and mercy are . . .

3. The word or phrase from today's liturgy that I want to ponder this week is . . .

Discussion

For discussion between candidates and sponsors:

1. DEEDS DONE IN DARKNESS	DEEDS DONE IN LIGHT

2. The ways I participate in these deeds of darkness are . . .

3. The ways I participate in these deeds of light are . . .

My prayer is . . .

Reflection

1. Words, phrases, and feelings I experienced in today's liturgy are . . .

2. An occasion in my life when forgiveness was offered to me before I even asked for it was . . .

   • Who was involved?

   • How did I respond to the offer of forgiveness?

   • How did this offer make me feel?

Discussion

For discussion between candidates and sponsors:

1. When in your life have you been the prodigal son, squandering your possessions, time, and talents on things that did not matter?

2. When in your life have you been the older son, angry that the sinner has been so easily forgiven, wanting the sinner to be punished severely for the sins, perhaps never receiving forgiveness yourself?

3. When in your life have you been the father, wanting to offer forgiveness to another so much that you offer it even before the other can say "I'm sorry"?

4. What does this parable tell you about God and about Jesus Christ, who loves you so much that before you were even born, he died for you?

My prayer is . . .

Reflection

1. The one or two things from this Liturgy of the Word and Scrutiny which stood out for me or touched me the most were . . .

2. This Scrutiny Rite proclaims that God is . . .

   Jesus is . . .

   grace is . . .

3. The experience of hearing our struggles prayed in the midst of the community was . . .

Discussion

For a discussion between elect and godparents and candidates and sponsors:

1. In what ways are you entombed from living a new way?

2. What keeps you from coming out of the tomb when Jesus calls your name?

3. Do you want to come out? Do you want to be freer? What would this mean to you?

4. How do you sense that Jesus is the resurrection and the life for you *now*?

My prayer is . . .

Reflection

1. Today's liturgy spoke to me or touched me in this way . . .

2. The way(s) I am being called to die in order to rise are . . .

3. The word or phrase from today's liturgy that I want to ponder this week is . . .

Discussion

For discussion between candidates and sponsors:

1. In what ways do I bring others to see Jesus?

2. When do I find it easy to follow Jesus?

3. When do I find it difficult to follow Jesus?

4. In what ways am I attempting to make this world heaven and losing sight of eternal life?

My prayer is . . .

Reflection

1. Words, phrases, and feelings I experienced in today's liturgy are . . .

2. For what sin could I be brought forth before God?

3. This week I want to ponder the words of Jesus to the woman and what they mean for me, which is . . .

Discussion

For discussion between candidates and sponsors:

1. Recall who or what prompted you to approach this parish to inquire about the Catholic faith.

2. In what ways is your faith journey like the race that Paul describes in his letter to the Philippians?

3. Describe the training you need in order to continue the race.

4. Ponder the finish line, not at the end of this process, but in heaven.

My prayer is . . .

Reflection

1. For me the experience of today's liturgy was . . .

2. Words, phrases, and feelings from today's liturgy that I cherish are . . .

3. The liturgy today proclaimed Christ . . .

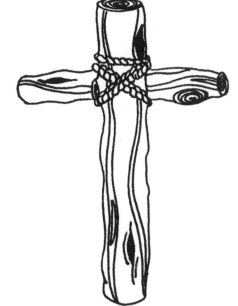

Discussion

For discussion between elect and godparents and candidates and sponsors:

1. What is becoming clearer to me about having a relationship with Jesus Christ is . . .

2. My relationship with Jesus involves . . .

3. For me to be claimed by Christ in baptism means . . .

4. The ways in which I have already begun to embrace discipleship are . . .

5. The greatest challenge to my ever deepening relationship with Christ will be . . .

My prayer is . . .

Reflection

1. For me the experience of today's liturgy was . . .

2. Words, phrases, and feelings from today's liturgy that I cherish are . . .

3. The liturgy today proclaimed Christ . . .

Discussion

For discussion between elect and godparents and candidates and sponsors:

Choose one of the images or events from the Passion narrative. Reflect on it using these questions as a guide:

- Where are you?

- Who are you seeing?

- Who or what are you hearing?

- What are you feeling?

- You have a conversation with Jesus. Summarize what Jesus says to you.

- Summarize what you say to Jesus.

My prayer is . . .

Reflection

1. For me the experience of today's liturgy was . . .

2. Words, phrases, and feelings from today's liturgy that I cherish are . . .

3. The liturgy today proclaimed Christ . . .

Discussion

For discussion between elect and godparents and candidates and sponsors:

1. With which person in the Passion narrative do you identify with and why?

2. What is becoming clearer to you about the meaning of discipleship?

3. As you approach the time of your baptism or renewal of your baptism, for what do you pray?

My prayer is . . .

Reflection

1. What did you observe about tonight's liturgy?

2. What did you hear in the liturgy?

3. What is the message proclaimed in tonight's liturgy?

4. Who does the message console? Who does it challenge?

5. I choose to wash the feet of . . .

   I refuse to wash the feet of . . .

   I allow . . . to wash my feet.

   I refuse to allow . . . to wash my feet.

Reflection

1. What did you observe about today's liturgy?

2. What did you hear in the liturgy?

3. What is the message proclaimed in today's liturgy?

4. Who does the message console? Who does it challenge?

5. The cross in my life is . . .

6. I am called to embrace this cross by . . .

7. My cross is a cross of victory, or my cross is a cross of suffering, because . . .

Reflection Questions

Identify ways that you have opened to God in your life. Be concrete. Look within yourself, in your family life, your work life, and your spiritual journey of conversion. You might find these questions helpful:

- How have I become more patient in my family and at work?

- Which areas of my life do I have a more positive attitude about?

- What are some ways that I take care of myself spiritually, physically, emotionally, and intellectually?

- What resentments have I been able to work through?

- What relationships have I worked toward forgiveness?

- What addictions have I been able to overcome?

- How often do I feel the presence of God? How often do I pray?

- How have I been able to surrender the difficult things in my life to God?

Now, take your time in identifying the areas in your life where you still feel that you hold out—name those barriers that prevent you from opening totally to God. Use the questions listed below to help you discover those things, which lie hidden in the recesses of your heart:

- When have I been stubborn, needing to control and have my own way?

- How do I envy those with whom I work or those among my circles of family and friends?

- What role does gossip and judgment of others play in my life?

- What is the root cause of my anger and inability to forgive?

- What in my life controls me?

- What secret guilt or hidden sin do I wish to open before the Lord?

- What about myself causes me inner struggle?

- What attitudes cause me to live in havoc instead of harmony?

Allow God to reveal to you those things which need to be brought into the light. Sit silently. When you are so moved, begin to write, letting your inner voice speak through the words you write on the page. Take all this to God's loving embrace.

Preparation

Pray to God, and examine your conscience in light of the Gospel (see Handout 24, Examination of Conscience). The priest who will hear your confession is also praying to the Holy Spirit that he will reflect the love and wisdom of Jesus to you.

Receiving the Penitent

When you go to the priest, you may either sit facing him or kneel behind a screen that is placed to his side. He will greet you and you will make the Sign of the Cross together, saying, "In the name of the Father, and of the Son, and of the Holy Spirit." The priest will speak some words of encouragement. If he does not know you, be sure to tell him at this time that you are a candidate for the sacraments or reception into the Church, that this is your first confession, and anything else that you think might help him. In celebrations of Reconciliation after this one, you would tell the priest at this time in the rite how long it has been since your last confession.

Reading of the Word of God

The priest may read a brief passage of Scripture or ask you to read one that he gives you. If he omits this, it is with the understanding that you have already read the Word of God in preparation for the sacrament.

Confession of Sins

At this time, you will tell, or confess, your sins to the priest. If you are uncertain about anything, he will help you. When you are finished, he will offer you counsel and give you an act of penance to perform. This may take the form of prayer, self-denial, or some work of mercy that expresses love of neighbor.

The Prayer of the Penitent and Absolution by the Priest

The priest will invite you to express sorrow for your sins and your resolution to begin a new life by praying a prayer of contrition, such as one of these or one in your own words:

My God,
I am sorry for my sins with all my heart.
In choosing to do wrong
and failing to do good,
I have sinned against you
whom I should love above all things.
I firmly intend, with your help,
to do penance,
to sin no more,
and to avoid whatever leads me to sin.
Our Savior, Jesus Christ,
suffered and died for us.
In his name, my God, have mercy.

—or—

Lord Jesus,
you chose to be called the friend of sinners.
By your saving death and resurrection
free me from my sins.
May your peace take root in my heart
and bring forth a harvest
of love, holiness, and truth.

—or—

Wash me from my guilt
and cleanse me from my sin.
I acknowledge my offense;
my sin is before me always. (Psalm 50:4–5)
—Taken from the Rite of Penance, 45

The priest will then extend his hand(s) over you and pronounce the formula of absolution, which always concludes with the words:

> *I absolve you from your sins in the name of the Father, and of the Son, and of the Holy Spirit.*

As he says the final words, he will make the Sign of the Cross over you. You respond, "Amen."

Proclamation of Praise and Dismissal of the Penitent

After receiving pardon, you may praise the mercy of God as follows:

Priest: *Give thanks to the Lord, for he is good.*

Your response: *His mercy endures forever.*

The priest will then dismiss you.

RITE OF RECONCILIATION OF SEVERAL PENITENTS WITH INDIVIDUAL CONFESSION AND ABSOLUTION

The elements of the celebration of the Rite of Reconciliation are:

Introductory Rites

    Song

    Greeting

    Introduction

    Opening Prayer

Celebration of the Word of God

    First Reading

    Responsorial Psalm

    Second Reading

    Gospel Acclamation

    Gospel

    Homily

    Examination of Conscience

Rite of Reconciliation

    General Confession of Sins ("I confess to Almighty God . . ." or some similar prayer)

    Litany or Song

    Lord's Prayer

    Individual Confession and Absolution

    During the time for individual confession, those who choose to do so go to a priest (usually several confessors are available), confess their sins, and receive absolution as described above. All the other elements of individual confession are omitted. If the confessor you choose does not know you, however, before you confess you should mention that you are a candidate for the sacraments or for reception into the Church and that this is your first confession.

    Proclamation of Praise for God's Mercy

    Concluding Rite of Thanksgiving

Concluding Rite

    Blessing

    Dismissal

EXAMINATION OF CONSCIENCE

As we come to know and experience God's great love for us, we become more aware of the ways we have sinned against that love, which calls us to live as true "children of light." By prayerfully reflecting on the following questions, you may be helped to call to mind sinful deeds and patterns in your life for which you want to ask God's forgiveness today. This examination of conscience is abridged from the Rite of Penance and can help to prepare for reception of the sacrament of Penance. (For an outline of the celebration of the sacrament see Handout 23.)

The Lord says, "You shall love the Lord God with your whole heart."

1. Is my heart set on God, so that I really love him above all things? Or am I more concerned with things of this world?

2. Is my faith in God firm and secure? Am I wholehearted in accepting the Church's teaching? Have I been careful to grow in my understanding of the faith? Have I always been strong and fearless in professing my faith in God and in the Church? Have I been willing to be known as a Christian in private and public life?

3. When I pray, do I really raise my mind and heart to God or is it a matter of words only? Do I offer God my difficulties, my joys, and my sorrows? Do I turn to God in time of temptation?

4. Do I have love and reverence for God's name? Have I offended him in blasphemy, swearing falsely, or taking his name in vain? Have I shown disrespect for the Blessed Virgin Mary and the saints?

5. Do I keep Sundays and feast days holy by taking a full part, with attention and devotion, in the liturgy?

6. Are there false gods, such as money, superstition, spiritism, or other occult practices, that I worship by giving them greater attention and deeper trust than I give to God?

The Lord says, "Love one another as I have loved you."

1. Do I have a genuine love for my neighbors? Or do I use them for my own ends or do to them what I would not want done to myself? Have I given grave scandal by my words or actions?

2. In my family life, have I contributed to the well-being and happiness of the rest of my family by patience and genuine love? Have I shown proper respect to parents by giving them help in their spiritual and material needs? Have I been careful to give a Christian upbringing to my children and to help them by good example and by exercising authority as a parent? Have I been faithful to my husband (or wife) in my heart and in my relations with others?

3. Do I share my possessions with the less fortunate? Do I do my best to help the victims of oppression, misfortune, and poverty? Or do I look down on my neighbor, especially the poor, the sick, the elderly, strangers, and people of other races?

4. Do I share in the apostolic and charitable works of the Church and in the life of my parish? Have I helped to meet the needs of the Church and of the world and prayed for them?

5. Am I concerned for the good and prosperity of the human community in which I live, or do I spend my life caring only for myself? Do I share to the best of my ability in the work of promoting justice, morality, harmony, and love in human relations? Have I done my duty as a citizen? Have I paid my taxes?

6. In my work or profession, am I just, hardworking, and honest, serving society out of love for others? Have I paid a fair wage to my employees? Have I been faithful to my promises and contracts?

7. Have I obeyed legitimate authority and given it due respect?

8. If I am in a position of responsibility or authority, do I use this for my own advantage or for the good of others in a spirit of service?

9. Have I been truthful and fair, or have I injured others by deceit, calumny, detraction, rash judgment, or violation of a secret?

10. Have I done violence to others by damage to life or limb, reputation, honor, or material possessions? Have I involved them in loss? Have I been responsible for advising an abortion or procuring one? Have I kept up hatred for others? Am I estranged from others through quarrels, enmity, insults, or anger? Have I been guilty of refusing to testify to the innocence of another because of selfishness?

11. Have I stolen the property of others? Have I desired it unjustly or inordinately? Have I made restitution of other people's property and made good their loss?

12. If I have been injured, have I been ready to make peace for the love of Christ and to forgive, or do I harbor hatred and the desire for revenge?

Christ our Lord says, "Be perfect as your Father is perfect."

1. Where is my life really leading me? Is the hope of eternal life my inspiration? Have I tried to grow in the life of the Spirit? Have I been anxious to control my vices, my bad inclinations and passions, for example, envy, love of food and drink? Have I been proud and boastful, thinking myself better in the sight of God and despising others as less important than myself? Have I imposed my will on others, without respecting their freedom and rights?

2. What use have I made of time, of health and strength, of the gifts God has given me to be used like the talents in the Gospel? Have I been lazy and too given to leisure?

3. Have I been patient in accepting the sorrows and disappointments of life?

4. Have I kept my senses and my whole body pure and chaste? Have I dishonored my body by fornication, impurity, unworthy conversation or thoughts, evil desires or actions? Have I given in to sensuality? Have I indulged in reading, conversation, shows, and entertainments that offend against Christian and human decency? Have I encouraged others to sin by my own failures to maintain high standards? Have I been faithful to the moral law in my married life?

5. Have I gone against my conscience out of fear or hypocrisy?

6. Have I always tried to act in the true freedom of God according to the law of the Spirit, or am I a slave to the forces within me?

PRAYER OF THANKSGIVING

Leader: *We give thanks, Yahweh. We have shared our stories—stories of lives filled with your constant care and presence. As we face the mission of carrying your Good News to all people, remove our fears and inspire us with the energetic fire of the Holy Spirit that your Word may inspire generations to come.*

Assembly: *Our hearts are grateful to you, Yahweh, whose name resounds throughout the universe.*

Leader: *We give thanks, Yahweh! Your compassion for us has led us to care for one another and to commit ourselves to work together in serving the needs of others. Teach us to serve without arrogance or the need for recognition, to heal with humility and a gentle touch, and to offer help with a heart open to receive the help of others. Fill us with love and empower us to reconcile your people and your world that your presence in us might transform our communities, country, and world.*

Assembly: *Our hearts are grateful to you, Yahweh, whose name resounds throughout the universe.*

Leader: *We give thanks, Yahweh! The Good News, made real in the person of Jesus, reveals to us, more clearly, who you are. You sent your Word to dwell with us that our words might reach our brothers and sisters in every nation, culture, and society with the Gospel. Let your Word not be spoken in vain. Let your Word yield a rich harvest. Let your Word accomplish all you have begun in our hearts this day.*

Assembly: *Our hearts are grateful to you, Yahweh, whose name resounds throughout the universe.*

Leader: *We give thanks, Yahweh! As we discover, once again, the power of the Paschal Mystery—the dying and rising of Jesus—we pray that the power of the eucharistic table will continually renew, refresh, and empower us with a fervor for Jesus' mission, bringing Good News to the poor, the imprisoned, the blind, the marginalized, and the unclean. May all be welcomed at your table and in our hearts and communities so that when we join you at the banquet of heaven, we might also be welcomed.*

Assembly: *Our hearts are grateful to you, Yahweh, whose Name resounds throughout the universe.*

Leader: *We give thanks, Yahweh! Today, we have discovered anew the presence and power of your Spirit. Your Spirit has preserved us as a People of God throughout history. Your Spirit has inspired prophets and preachers, setting a fire on this earth. Your Spirit has led us through the dark night of tragedy and crises, opening us even more to receive your love. We pray that this Holy Spirit will give us the courage to speak truth, purify us of all prejudice, strengthen us when we are weak and weary, and grace us with joy as we walk the journey of our call to discipleship.*

Assembly: *Our hearts are grateful to you, Yahweh, whose name resounds throughout the universe.*